# DOORS AND WINDOWS

*Other Publications:*

PLANET EARTH
COLLECTOR'S LIBRARY OF THE CIVIL WAR
LIBRARY OF HEALTH
CLASSICS OF THE OLD WEST
THE EPIC OF FLIGHT
THE GOOD COOK
THE SEAFARERS
THE ENCYCLOPEDIA OF COLLECTIBLES
THE GREAT CITIES
WORLD WAR II
THE WORLD'S WILD PLACES
THE TIME-LIFE LIBRARY OF BOATING
HUMAN BEHAVIOR
THE ART OF SEWING
THE OLD WEST
THE EMERGENCE OF MAN
THE AMERICAN WILDERNESS
THE TIME-LIFE ENCYCLOPEDIA OF GARDENING
LIFE LIBRARY OF PHOTOGRAPHY
THIS FABULOUS CENTURY
FOODS OF THE WORLD
TIME-LIFE LIBRARY OF AMERICA
TIME-LIFE LIBRARY OF ART
GREAT AGES OF MAN
LIFE SCIENCE LIBRARY
THE LIFE HISTORY OF THE UNITED STATES
TIME READING PROGRAM
LIFE NATURE LIBRARY
LIFE WORLD LIBRARY
FAMILY LIBRARY:
   HOW THINGS WORK IN YOUR HOME
   THE TIME-LIFE BOOK OF THE FAMILY CAR
   THE TIME-LIFE FAMILY LEGAL GUIDE
   THE TIME-LIFE BOOK OF FAMILY FINANCE

This volume is part of a series offering homeowners
detailed instructions on repairs, construction
and improvements they can undertake themselves.

HOME REPAIR
AND IMPROVEMENT

# DOORS AND WINDOWS

BY THE EDITORS OF
TIME-LIFE BOOKS

TIME-LIFE BOOKS
ALEXANDRIA, VIRGINIA

Time-Life Books Inc.
is a wholly owned subsidiary of
**TIME INCORPORATED**

Founder Henry R. Luce 1898-1967

Editor-in-Chief Henry Anatole Grunwald
President J. Richard Munro
Chairman of the Board Ralph P. Davidson
Executive Vice President Clifford J. Grum
Chairman, Executive Committee James R. Shepley
Editorial Director Ralph Graves
Group Vice President, Books Joan D. Manley
Vice Chairman Arthur Temple

**TIME-LIFE BOOKS INC.**

Editor George Constable
Executive Editor George Daniels
Director of Design Louis Klein
Board of Editors Dale M. Brown, Thomas H. Flaherty Jr., William Frankel,
Thomas A. Lewis, Martin Mann, John Paul Porter,
Gerry Schremp, Gerald Simons, Kit van Tulleken
Director of Administration David L. Harrison
Director of Research Carolyn L. Sackett
Director of Photography Dolores Allen Littles

President Carl G. Jaeger
Executive Vice Presidents John Steven Maxwell, David J. Walsh
Vice Presidents George Artandi, Stephen L. Bair, Peter G. Barnes,
Nicholas Benton, John L. Canova, Beatrice T. Dobie,
James L. Mercer

**HOME REPAIR AND IMPROVEMENT**

Editor William Frankel
Designer Anne Masters

Editorial Staff for Doors and Windows
Picture Editor Adrian Allen
Text Editors David Thiemann, Richard Flanagan, John Manners,
Bob Menaker
Writers Lynn R. Addison, Megan Barnett, Thierry Bright-Saignier,
Stephen Brown, Alan Epstein, Steven J. Forbis,
Leslie Marshall, Brooke Stoddard, William Worsley
Associate Designer Kenneth E. Hancock
Copy Coordinator Margery duMond
Art Assistants George Bell, Lorraine D. Rivard, Richard Whiting
Picture Coordinator Renée DeSandies
Editorial Assistant Susanne S. Trice

Editorial Operations

Production Director Feliciano Madrid
Assistant Peter A. Inchauteguiz
Copy Processing Gordon E. Buck
Quality Control Director Robert L. Young
Assistant James J. Cox
Associates Daniel J. McSweeney, Michael G. Wight
Art Coordinator Anne B. Landry
Copy Room Director Susan Galloway Goldberg
Assistants Celia Beattie, Ricki Tarlow

Correspondents: Elisabeth Kraemer (Bonn); Margot
Hapgood, Dorothy Bacon, Lesley Coleman (London);
Susan Jonas, Lucy T. Voulgaris (New York); Maria
Vincenza Aloisi, Josephine du Brusle (Paris); Ann
Natanson (Rome). Valuable assistance was also
provided by: Judy Aspinall (London); Carolyn T.
Chubet, Miriam Hsia, Christina Lieberman (New
York); Mimi Murphy (Rome).

THE CONSULTANTS: Charles Hamilton, a carpenter and
construction supervisor, has specialized in custom re-
modeling and restoration in the Washington, D.C., area
for more than three decades.

John Talbert, the masonry consultant for this book, is a
bricklayer and estimator for a masonry contractor in Silver Spring, Maryland. His firm has been awarded the
masonry craftsmanship award of the Washington, D.C.,
Building Congress.

Roswell W. Ard is a consulting structural engineer and a
professional home inspector in northern Michigan. He
has written professional papers on wood-frame construction techniques.

Harris Mitchell, special consultant for Canada, has
worked in the field of home repair and improvement for
more than two decades. He is Homes editor of Today
magazine, writes a syndicated newspaper column, "You
Wanted to Know," and is the author of a number of books
on home improvement.

For information about any Time-Life book, please write:
Reader Information
Time-Life Books
541 North Fairbanks Court
Chicago, Illinois 60611

Library of Congress Cataloguing in Publication Data
Time-Life Books.
   Doors and windows.
   (Home repair and improvement; v. 14)
   Includes index.
   1. Doors.   2. Windows.   II. Title.
TH2270.T55      1978      643.7      78-1384
ISBN 0-8094-2408-8
ISBN 0-8094-2407-X lib. bdg.
ISBN 0-8094-2406-1 retail ed.

# Contents

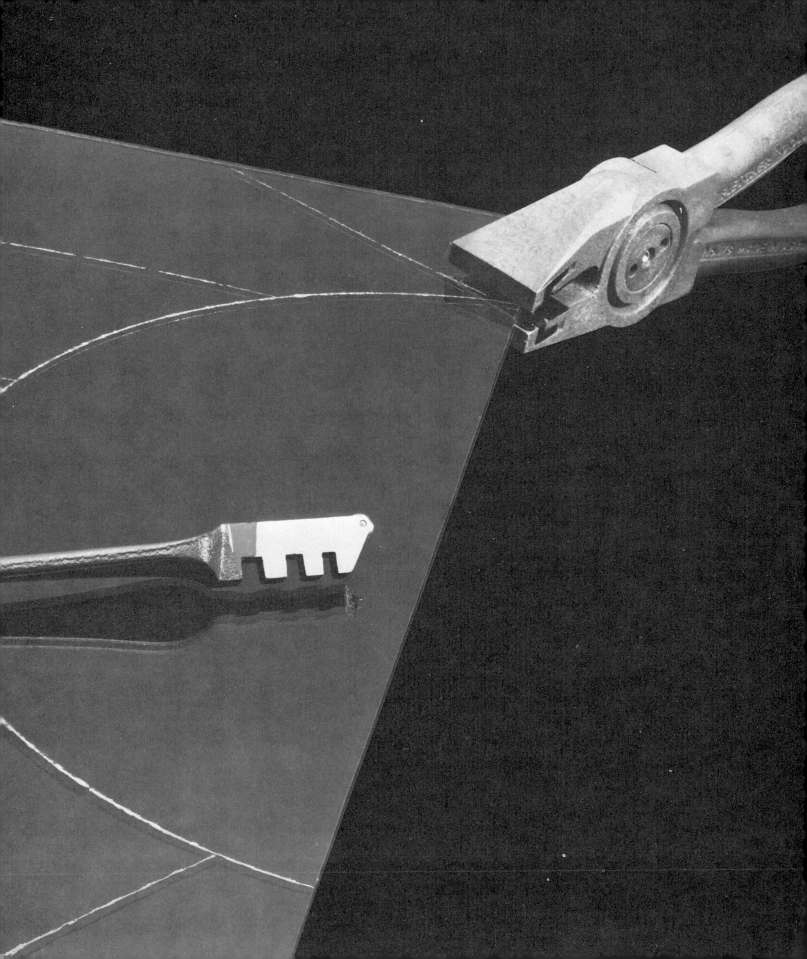

# Curing the Common Ailments

Windows and doors are the Achilles' heel of a house—and no wonder. These covered holes in the house walls must seal out wind, rain, snow and ice, but they must also break the seal at the touch of a hand. The walls are massive and stationary; the doors and windows, the only moving parts in the structure of the house, are intricate little machines that are designed to open and close thousands of times a year. And while the sheathing and siding of the walls are carefully lapped and layered against moisture, the doors and windows abound in cracks and crevices where heat, cold and moisture can enter and rot can begin. It is all a great paradox: an opening, vulnerable to all the vagaries of weather, has been deliberately set into a shelter that has been built to keep the weather out.

Every door and window is a compromise between these conflicting demands. Like most compromises it eventually breaks down—and doors and windows do in fact require frequent maintenance. The most common repairs are straightforward, once you know how to get at the problem. Broken sash cords and crank mechanisms, for example, can be replaced; the cords of a balky Venetian blind can be rethreaded; the hinges of a sagging door can be retightened. You can cure more serious ailments with tricks handed down through generations of carpenters. If need be, you can replace a broken divider in an antique window sash by cutting new joints to match the old ones and fastening the new piece with wooden dowels; somewhat more simply, you can adjust the parts of a window frame to free a sticky sash, straighten a doorjamb without removing it from its place, or cut a curved pane of glass (opposite) for an exotic window.

Some doors and windows are so rotted, warped or irredeemably shabby as to be beyond repair. The simplest remedy in this case is to replace them with modern prefabricated units that come complete with finish frames and built-in weather stripping. If the old door or window is a standard size, you can remove it and fasten a new one into the same rough opening in a matter of a few hours, without altering the structure of the wall. The only tools you will require are a hammer, a carpenter's level and perhaps a screwdriver.

If you cannot match the size of the old unit, you can save work and time by adapting its opening to a slightly smaller modern unit—usually this can be done with strips of 1-inch lumber nailed to the wall studs at each side. If you decide to install a larger unit, however—a sliding glass double door in place of a single wooden door, for example—you will have to shore the walls and joists temporarily above the opening, enlarge the hole in the wall and construct a new rough framework to support the door unit—a procedure described in Chapter 2 of this book.

# Why Windows Stick—and How to Free Them

Like the walls of a house, windows must withstand rain, snow, wind and sun. But walls are solid, permanent barriers, protected from the weather by layers of siding, building paper, sheathing and insulation; a movable window is a relatively fragile machine, fitted with gears, springs, counterweights or rollers to make it open and close. Like all machines, windows at times move reluctantly and occasionally freeze outright.

The basic parts of a window are almost always the same. It has glazed sashes that slide or swing open, a frame, and narrow strips at the sides and top of the frame to hold the sash in place. But each type of window has a different mechanism and a few special parts, and in each type the parts fit together in a different fashion and serve slightly different functions.

Wooden windows like the ones shown on these pages are the easiest to repair because the parts are assembled with carpentry techniques. Metal windows, less common because only costly ones insulate as well as wood, generally combine the functions of the several parts of a wooden window frame in one-piece metal channels.

The most common cause of balky sashes—and the easiest to cure—is a layer of old paint and dirt that narrows the channel between the stops until the sash binds. This layer can be removed with a wood chisel and sandpaper (page 10), though in some stubborn cases you may have to remove the sash (page 12) to do a thorough job.

If the channel is clean but the sash jams partway open or will not stay open at all, the mechanism is probably at fault. You can repair an older double-hung window, whose weight is counterbalanced by a pulley and a metal or masonry bob, by simply replacing a cord (pages 12-13). In newer double-hung windows, the counterbalance is one of several types of spring devices that generally cannot be repaired and must be replaced if faulty (pages 14-16). Casement and awning windows can be fixed by replacing the crank assembly (pages 17-18).

If the sash sticks in a window with clean channels and a sound mechanism, check the jamb with a straightedge, to see whether it is bowed, and slip a piece of paper along the joints between the stops and the sash, to see whether the sash is binding there. Once you find the point of friction, you may be able to free the sash by driving the jamb or stop away from it slightly with a block of wood and a hammer (page 10, bottom).

A sash that will not budge may be literally nailed—by long-forgotten nails. In order to remove finishing nails, drive them completely through the sash with a nail set; pull any large-headed nails with carpenter's nippers (page 28); then try to free the sash by the techniques described on page 11.

If none of these standard remedies works, you will have to dismantle the window. A sash that binds against a stop can be freed by removing the stop (page 28), moving it back slightly and renailing it to the jamb—but be sure to move the stop only a fraction of an inch, or the sash will rattle in the wind. When a jamb is badly bowed, something behind it—wallboard, plaster, shims or insulation—is probably forcing it out of line. In this case, remove the casing, the apron and the stool (pages 28 and 33), pull out the shims in the vicinity of the trouble, and then square, level and plumb the window frame as you would when installing a new window. Do not try to use the easy trick of removing the sash and planing down its sides—no matter how little wood you shave away, you will almost certainly end up with a rattling sash.

## The Four Basic Window Types

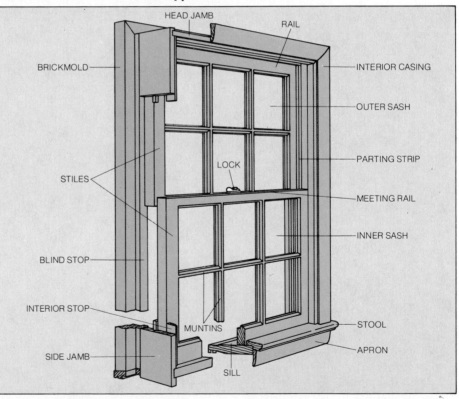

HEAD JAMB · RAIL · BRICKMOLD · INTERIOR CASING · OUTER SASH · PARTING STRIP · LOCK · MEETING RAIL · STILES · INNER SASH · BLIND STOP · INTERIOR STOP · MUNTINS · STOOL · APRON · SIDE JAMB · SILL

**A double-hung window.** The frame consists of two side jambs; a head, or top, jamb; and a two-piece bottom of sill and stool. Sliding inside the jambs are an inner and an outer sash. (In a single-hung window only the lower, or inner, sash moves.) The sashes are held by three thin pieces: a blind stop on the outside, a parting strip between the sashes, and an interior stop. Each sash has two horizontal rails and two vertical stiles. Many sashes are divided by muntins, which secure panes of glass. Inside, a horizontal stool fills the bottom of the frame and an apron fits underneath it; outside, the bottom of the frame is filled by a finish sill. The joints between the jambs and the wall indoors are covered by three pieces of interior casing; the joints between the jambs and the exterior siding are covered by exterior casing, called brickmold.

**A casement window.** These sashes, hung singly or in pairs, have hinges mounted to top and bottom rails; because the sashes swing outward there are no exterior stops. In most modern casement windows the sash is moved by a mechanism called an operator, which consists of a geared crank and an extension arm that slides in a track on the lower rail; in many older windows, the sash is simply pushed or pulled by hand or by a hand-held rod. The latch and lock are mounted on the stile and side jamb opposite the hinges. Casement windows often have no stool or apron; instead, a bottom stop and a fourth piece of interior casing complete the frame.

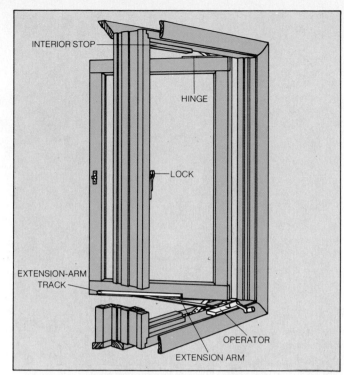

INTERIOR STOP

HINGE

LOCK

EXTENSION-ARM TRACK

OPERATOR

EXTENSION ARM

**An awning window.** The sash, hinged near the top of each stile, swings out at the bottom, ventilating a room while blocking rain. In this widely used design, the sash is moved by an operator with two scissor arms that fold against the sill when the window is closed. Like a casement window, the awning window often has interior casing on all four sides.

The construction of a hopper window, which swings out at the top, is virtually identical to that of an awning window.

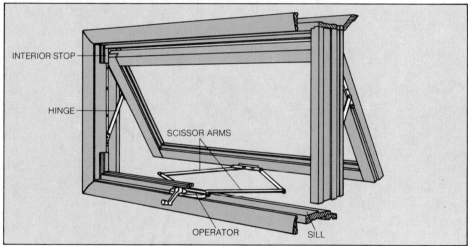

INTERIOR STOP

HINGE

SCISSOR ARMS

OPERATOR

SILL

**A sliding window.** Sashes slide horizontally, generally on plastic rollers along the channels of metal or vinyl jamb liners at the top and bottom of the window frame. A latch and lock are mounted on the meeting stiles. In most models, the sashes can be removed without dismantling the window frame—you simply lift them up and tilt the bottom rail out of its channel.

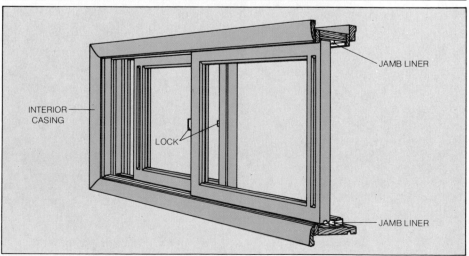

JAMB LINER

INTERIOR CASING

LOCK

JAMB LINER

9

# Easing a Tight Sash

**Cleaning the channels.** On wooden or metal channels, run a chisel, flat side out, along the surfaces touched by the sash. Clean the jambs first, then the sides of the stops and the parting strips, if any. Apply steady pressure to pare away dirt and paint. Sand cleaned wooden channels. Plastic channels and weather stripping of any sort should be cleaned with steel wool, since a chisel might damage the surfaces.

**Lubricating the channels.** A block of household paraffin run up and down the channels three or four times will apply a light coat of wax to wooden jambs, stops and parting strips. But if you intend to paint the window, be sure to do that job first, before you wax the channels. Silicone spray lubricant can also be applied to wooden parts, and it is better than wax as a lubricant for metal or plastic window parts.

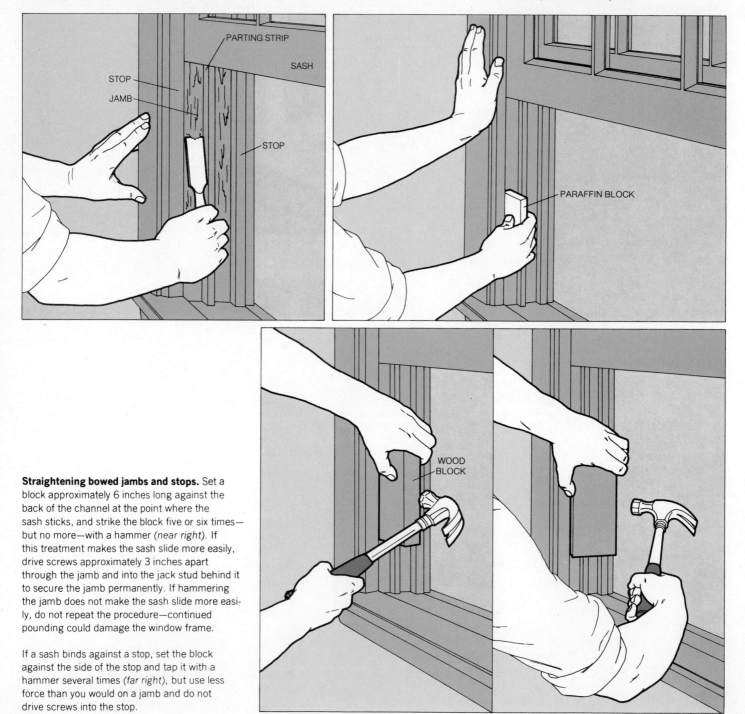

**Straightening bowed jambs and stops.** Set a block approximately 6 inches long against the back of the channel at the point where the sash sticks, and strike the block five or six times—but no more—with a hammer (*near right*). If this treatment makes the sash slide more easily, drive screws approximately 3 inches apart through the jamb and into the jack stud behind it to secure the jamb permanently. If hammering the jamb does not make the sash slide more easily, do not repeat the procedure—continued pounding could damage the window frame.

If a sash binds against a stop, set the block against the side of the stop and tap it with a hammer several times (*far right*), but use less force than you would on a jamb and do not drive screws into the stop.

## Freeing a Frozen Sash

**Breaking a paint seal.** Force a wide-blade putty knife into the joint between the sash and the stop. Work the knife around both sides of the sash, then force it into the joint between the sash and the stool. If the sash still will not move, go outside the house and check the joint between the sash and the parting strip; repeat the procedure there if necessary.

**Prying open a double-hung window.** Force the blade of a heavy screwdriver between the sash and the jamb; if the sash has a groove for a sash cord, use it as the point of entry for the blade. Pry the sash away from the jamb, then repeat the procedure at the other side of the sash. Continue to work the sash to the right and left until you can slide it open.

**Prying the sash up from outside.** If all else fails, go outside the house and wedge a utility bar between the finish sill and the sash. Set a block of wood on the sill under the utility bar for leverage and pry the sash up, working first under the corners of the sash.

# Replacing a Broken Sash Cord

Without some kind of support, the sashes of a double-hung window would slide to the bottom of the window frame every time you raised them. The traditional support method, standard from the 1600s up to about 1950, uses a system of counterweights much like those of an elevator or a dumb-waiter. Two pulleys, one for each sash, are built into the top of each vertical window jamb; from the sides of the sashes, cords run over the pulleys to metal or masonry weights hidden within the jamb. This simple, reliable system has only one drawback: eventually a cord breaks and the sash jams in its channel or falls to the bottom of the window frame.

To replace the cords of the lower sash, generally the first to break, you must remove both the sash and a wooden access plate that covers the sash weight inside the jamb, then thread a new cord over the pulley and tie it to the sash and weight. (While you have the sash out, check the unbroken cord for wear; you may avoid trouble later by replacing it as well.) To get at the upper sash cords, first take out the lower sash and the parting strip between the sashes.

You can replace the broken cord with a length of new sash cord—do not use ordinary rope, which wears too quickly—or solve the problem permanently with sash chain, available at hardware stores. To use chain, however, you must have a metal pulley with a wide groove at the center: a pulley with a narrow groove is likely to jam the chain; a wooden pulley will splinter.

Sash weights are occasionally involved in seemingly unrelated window problems. Long nails driven through the casing or jamb can interfere with the weights, jamming the sash or leaving it unsupported; pull such nails with carpenter's nippers (page 28). And if sash cords stretch, so that the weights lie on the bottom of the window frame, a sash will not stay fully open. You need not replace a stretched cord; simply remove the sash and the access plate in the side jamb, then cut a few inches from the end of the cord and retie it to the weight.

**1 Removing the lower sash.** Pry off the stop (page 28) on the side of the window where the cord is broken. Then raise the sash slightly, angle it toward you and pull it sideways until the other side is free of its stop. Pull the knot at the sash end of the broken cord down with a pair of long-nose pliers, untie it and set the piece of cord aside. Pull out the knot at the end of the other cord from the other side of the sash in the same way but untie the knot, slip the cord out of the sash, tie a large knot in the end and guide this knot up until it rests against the pulley. Remove any weather stripping from the lower part of the jamb. If your window has interlocking weather stripping, which fits into a groove in the sash, remove the stop and have a helper raise the sash and hold it at the top of the window frame. Using carpenter's nippers, remove the nails that fasten the metal weather-stripping track; then carefully angle both the weather stripping and the sash out of the window frame.

**2 Taking out the access plate.** Remove the wood screws at the top and bottom of the access plate and pry the plate out of the jamb with a wood chisel. Reach into the access hole revealed by the plate, take out the sash weight and untie the broken cord. Add 1 foot to the total length of the broken cord and cut a new cord or a chain to this length.

If the parting strip covers one edge of the access plate, remove the strip (opposite, bottom) before prying out the plate. If the access plate is completely concealed by paint, rap on the lower part of the sash channel with a hammer. When the outline of the plate appears, cut around it with a utility knife, then remove the screws and pry out the plate. If your window does not have an access plate, you will have to remove the casing (page 28) to get at the sash weight.

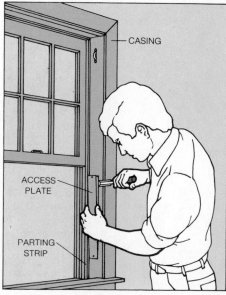

**3 Putting in the new cord.** Tie a bent eight-penny nail to a piece of string, tie the other end of the string to one end of the new sash cord, and feed the string over the pulley until the nail appears at the access hole; then pull the cord over the pulley and down to the access hole. Untie the string and tie the cord to the sash weight, leaving about 3 inches of surplus cord. Rest the sash on the sill and refasten the undamaged cord on the opposite side.

If you are using a sash chain, put a nail through a link at one end to keep the chain from slipping through the pulley and feed the other end over the pulley until it appears at the access hole. Put the end of the chain through the eye of the weight and fasten the loop with thin wire or with clips provided by the manufacturer.

**4 Attaching the new cord to the sash.** With the sash still resting on the sill, pull down on the new cord until the sash weight touches the pulley, then lower the weight about 2 inches and thread the cord into its groove in the sash. Tie a knot in the cord at the level of the hole in the side of the sash, cut off any extra cord and insert the knot in the hole. Hold the sash in its track and slide it all the way up; the bottom of the weight should be visible in the access hole, about

2 inches above the bottom of the window frame. If necessary, adjust the cord by retying it at the sash weight. Replace the access plate, the weather stripping (if any) and the stop; use short nails that will not touch the sash weight and do not drive any nails into the access plate.

To attach a sash chain, thread the chain into the groove in the sash and run wood screws through two of its links into the sash *(inset)*.

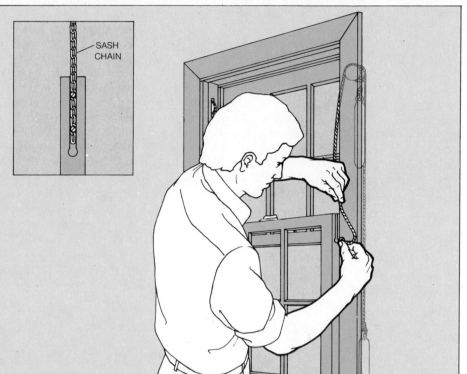

SASH CHAIN

## Removing the Upper Sash

**Pulling the parting strip.** After removing a side stop and the lower sash *(Step 1, opposite)*, lower the upper sash. Drill a pilot hole in the parting strip about 3 inches from the top and thread a short wood screw into it. Caution: do not run the screw clear through the strip into the jamb. Pull steadily on the screw with a pair of pliers until you can slip a wood chisel behind the end of the parting strip. From this point, pry the strip out a little at a time with the wood chisel, moving the chisel downward as the gap widens between the jamb and the parting strip. When the top half of the strip is free, slide the sash to the top of the window frame, then continue to pry out the lower half of the parting strip.

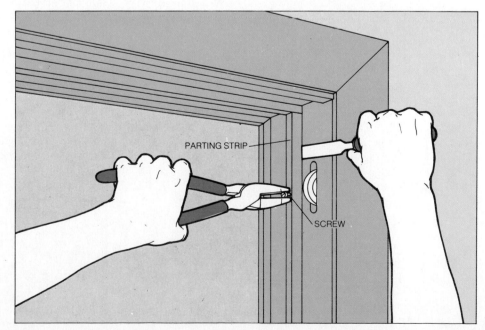

PARTING STRIP

SCREW

# Replacing Spring-Loaded Sash Balances

During the years after World War II, manufacturers of double-hung windows discarded the sash-weight balancing system described on page 12. In its place, they began to install several varieties of less expensive spring-loaded balances. The signs of a broken balance and of a broken sash-weight cord are the same—the sash either jams in its track or falls to the bottom of the window frame—but the remedies are different. A broken balance cannot be repaired. You must remove it and get an exact replacement at a hardware store or a window-repair shop.

The techniques for removing an old balance and installing a new one depend on the type of balance mechanism you already have. These mechanisms come in four general categories:

☐ Channel balances, which combine the functions of balances and weather stripping, have sheet-metal tracks nailed to the side jambs of the window frame. Tabs protruding from the tracks hold the sashes up; the tabs, in turn, are supported by tension springs hidden behind the tracks. In a channel repair job, always replace both the left and right balances; the act of removing the sashes usually bends both channels beyond repair.

☐ Tube balances are metal or plastic cylinders that fit into grooves in the sides of the sashes and are screwed to the tops of the jambs. Inside each cylinder, a spring-loaded spiral rod fastened to the bottom of the sash holds the sash up by a spring. The tension on the spring can be adjusted by turning the rod (page 15, Step 2), and this alone may free a sticky sash.

☐ Tape balances are spring-loaded drums fitted into pockets at the tops of the side jambs or the corners of the head jamb. Thin, flexible metal tapes, hooked to the sides of the sashes, unreel from the drums as the sashes are lowered.

☐ Cord balances—a spring-loaded variation of the old sash cord—fit into pockets in each corner of the head jamb, behind a vinyl jamb liner. Each balance contains one reel for the upper sash and one for the lower; a nylon cord runs from each reel to the side of a sash.

## Channel Balances

**1 Removing the channels.** With carpenter's nippers, pull the nails or staples that fasten the channels to the side jambs; then remove the interior stops, if any, from the side and head jambs (page 28) and slide both sashes to the middle of the window. Working at one channel while a helper works at the other, tilt the tops of both channels inward, let the bottoms slide partway outdoors from the window, and remove both the channels and the sashes as a single unit. Set the bottoms of the channels on the floor and, while your helper holds them upright against the sashes, slide the sashes up and out of the channels.

CHANNEL BALANCES

**2 Installing new channels.** While your helper holds the new channels upright on the floor, with the angles cut by the manufacturer at their bottoms matching the slant of the window's finish sill, slide the inner—that is, the bottom—sash into the channel tracks, then the outer sash. Working with the helper, lift the entire unit into the window frame, using the technique described in Step 1 (above). Position the channels against the blind stops of the window frame and fasten them to the side jambs with fourpenny galvanized nails inserted at the top and bottom of each track. Replace the interior stops.

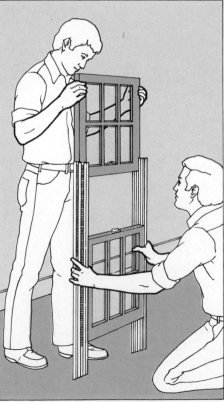

## Tube Balances

**1** **Removing the balance.** On the side of the window with the broken balance, remove both the stop *(page 28)* and the screw that fastens the top of the tube to the side jamb; then raise the sash about 8 inches, angle the side of the sash out of the window frame and support the sash on wooden blocks. If the spiral rod is fastened to the mounting bracket on the bottom edge of the sash with a detachable hook, unhook it; otherwise unscrew the bracket.

If your tube balances are built into channels like those shown opposite, remove the channels and sashes together *(opposite, Step 1)*.

**2** **Installing a new balance.** Set the new tube into its groove and screw the top of the tube to the side jamb. Pull the spiral rod down until it is fully extended, then tighten the spring inside the tube by turning the rod about four complete revolutions. Let the rod retract into the tube until you can screw the mounting bracket to the bottom of the sash.

Slide the sash up and down in its frame. If it creeps up when you release it, loosen the balance spring by turning the rod; if it creeps down, turn the rod to tighten the spring. When the balance is correct, replace the stop.

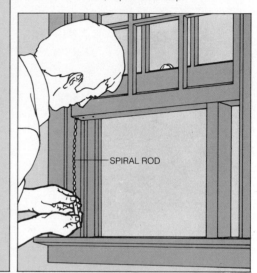

TUBE

MOUNTING BRACKET

SPIRAL ROD

## Tape Balances

**Replacing the drum.** On the side of the window with the broken balance, remove the stop *(page 28)* and angle the sash out of the frame; then unhook the end of the tape from the sash and feed it back into the tape drum. Remove the screws that secure the drum and pull it out of its pocket in the side or head jamb.

Slip the new tape balance into the jamb and fasten it with wood screws. Pull the end of the tape from the drum with long-nose pliers and hook it to the sash. Angle the sash back into the window frame and replace the stop.

TAPE BALANCE

## Cord Balances

**1 Removing the jamb liners.** With both sashes at the bottom of the window frame, remove the two screws that fasten the vinyl liner to the head jamb and pull out the liner *(below, top)*.

Raise both of the sashes and unscrew the lower of the two pieces of vinyl that make up the left jamb liner; always remove the left jamb liner, regardless of whether the left or the right balance is broken. Then gently bend the bottom of the liner toward the center of the window and pull the liner down and out *(below, bottom)*.

**2 Replacing the balance.** Lower the inner sash and angle the left side of the sash out of the window frame; unhook the balance cord and guide it up to its balance. Unhook the right-hand cord, guide it up to its balance and set the sash aside. Lower the outer sash, unfasten its cords similarly and set it aside.

Remove the two screws that secure the faulty balance in its pocket in the head jamb. Install a new balance, hook its cords to the sashes and replace the sashes and jamb liners.

# Working on Windows that Swing

A window sash designed to swing rather than slide can stick fast in paint or dirt at its edges, but it can then be freed by the remedies on pages 10-11. More often, it is the mechanism that moves the sash, not the sash itself, that binds. You may solve the problem by cleaning and lubricating the hinges and the accessible moving parts *(right)*. Otherwise you will have to remove and repair or replace the sash-moving mechanism, which is technically called the operator.

In both casement and awning windows, the operator is essentially the same. It consists of a metal housing, a shaft with a crank handle at one end and a worm gear at the other, and an extension arm (or, in an awning window, two scissor-like arms) pivoting in the housing at one end and linked to the bottom of the sash at the other. When the crank is turned, teeth at the pivot end of the arm or arms mesh with the worm gear, swinging the arm—and the sash—in or out.

If the grease inside the operator is thick with dirt, clogging the works, you can clean and relubricate the gears. But if the gears have become so worn that they do not mesh, then you will have to replace the entire operator with a new one. The replacement must match the old operator exactly and, on a casement window, it must move the sash in the same direction as the old one—to the right or to the left as viewed from inside the house. Most hardware stores stock some replacement operators, but you may have to send to the window manufacturer or to a specialty shop for the operator you need.

Repairing the crank handle or latch of a swinging window generally involves simply unscrewing the old part and installing a new one; the most difficult part of the job may be finding a matching part. The crank handle, which is secured by a setscrew, slides off its shaft; the latch is fastened to the jamb by screws. If the latch fails to pull the sash tight to the weather stripping, you can shim the latch as you would a hinge (page 23), by slipping a piece of either cardboard or sheet metal behind it.

**Lubricating the window.** On a casement window *(top)*, apply a few drops of household oil—or, for a better and longer-lasting job, an aerosol spray of silicone lubricant—to the hinges, the pivot of the latch and the joint between the crank handle and the operator. Open and close the window several times to work the lubricant into the joints. On an awning window *(bottom)*, lubricate the hinges, the joints between the scissor arms and the sash, the pivot joint in the middle of each scissor arm and the joint between the crank handle and the operator.

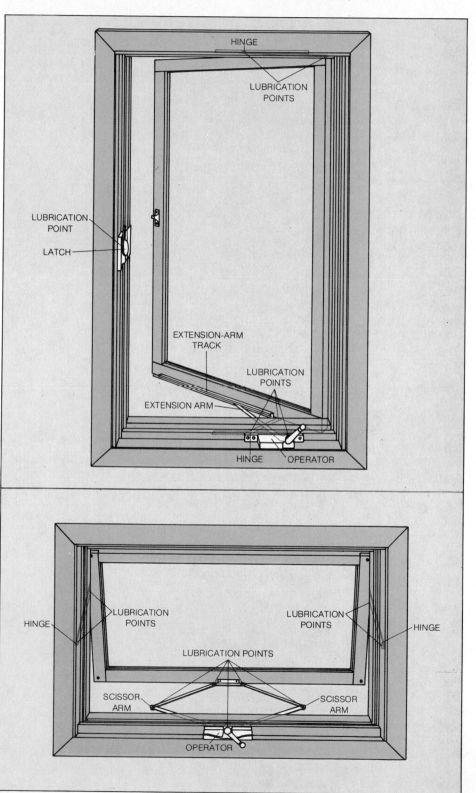

**Cleaning an extension-arm track.** Open the window fully and scrape hardened grease, paint and accumulated dirt from the track with a wire brush. Scrape away any remaining debris with an old screwdriver, taking special care to remove obstructions inside the lip of the track. Coat the inside of the track with a thin layer of silicone spray or petroleum jelly.

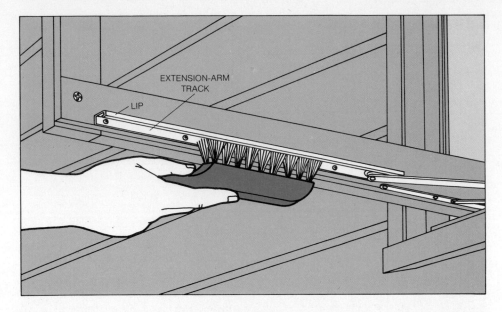

## Fixing a Cranky Operator

**1** **Unfastening the operator.** Open the window and remove the screws that fasten the operator to the jamb; if the screws are not visible, pry off the stop above the operator (*inset*) by the method on page 28 to gain access to them. On a casement window like the one pictured here, remove any screws or spring clips that hold the arm in the track at the bottom of the sash.

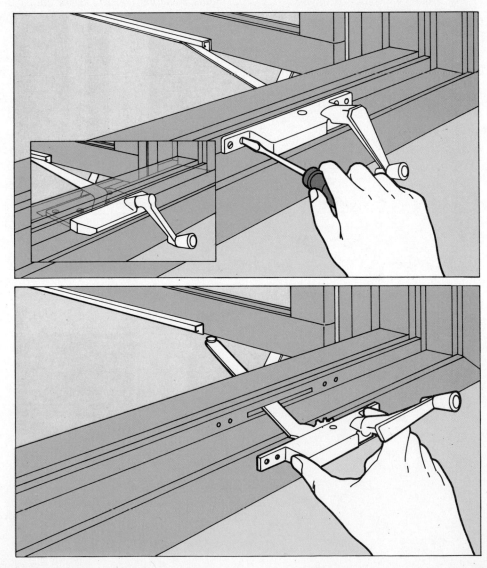

**2** **Removing the operator.** On a casement window, pull the crank mechanism inward, sliding the extension arm along its track until the end of the arm slips out of the track. Pull the arm completely through its slot in the window frame. On an awning window, unhook the scissor arms from the bracket at the bottom of the sash and pull the operator indoors.

Inspect the gear on the extension arm or arms. If the teeth are rounded or broken, install a new operator. If they have sharp, distinct edges, wash the housing out with kerosene to remove the old grease and let the operator dry completely. Coat metal gears lightly with petroleum jelly or graphite powder and turn the crank handle several times to spread the lubricant. Caution: do not lubricate nylon gears; if they do not work smoothly, replace the operator.

# The Age-old Language of Doors and Windows

*Muntin* and *astragal, dado* and *kerf*—the words sound like a witch's chant. In fact, these haunting terms stand for ordinary objects: the parts of a door or a window, and the joints and cuts that fit the parts together.

The ancient craft of joinery—that is, fine carpentry, such as that needed in constructing doors and windows—has evolved over the years, but much of its basic vocabulary remains essentially unchanged. Like the language of any skilled craft, the words in the following list are worth knowing for their economy and precision; properly understood, they tell you exactly what piece or cut is involved. And the derivations of some of these words yield fascinating glimpses into history.

APRON: The inside trim that lies flat against the wall beneath the interior window sill, more properly called the stool (*below*). It hangs like an apron over the joint between the stool and the wall and covers that gap.

ASTRAGAL: A strip on a double door that overlaps the gap between the two doors and prevents them from swinging past each other. The term comes from the Greek word for vertebra.

BRICKMOLD: Trim around the outside of the door or window. The term derives from a time when elegant windows were set in masonry walls, with a molding fitted against the brickwork.

CASING: or, in Great Britain, and sometimes in Canada, ARCHITRAVE: The trim around the top and sides of a window or door inside the house.

DADO: A rectangular groove across the width of a board, designed to accept the end of a second piece. The term comes from the Italian for die or cube.

FINISH FRAME: The stationary pieces immediately adjacent to the movable parts of a window or door. Those at the side and top are called jambs. The bottom piece on a window is the sill; on a door it is the threshold.

HEADER: A wooden beam across the top of a door or window, supporting the weight of the wall above. A steel, stone or concrete header is called a lintel.

JACK STUD: A vertical support that holds up the beam laid across the top of the opening for a window or door. The term is related to the mechanical jack, like the type used in car repair.

JAMB: A piece at the side or top of the frame around a window or door, adjoining the moving parts. The top piece is called the head jamb; the term jamb used alone usually refers to the side pieces. The word comes from the Latin *gamba,* meaning leg—the jambs are legs that straddle the opening.

KERF: The cut made by a saw blade. The word comes almost unchanged from the Old English *cyrf,* meaning "cut."

KING STUD: A full-height vertical support beside a window or door opening, flanking a shorter support, the jack stud, for the beam over the opening.

LIGHT: A window, a section of a divided window, or a pane set in a window.

MITER: An angle cut into an edge to make it fit a matching angle in another piece; many trim ends are cut at 45° angles to form a right-angle joint.

MORTISE: A recess cut in one piece to hold another. A shallow mortise is usually fitted with hardware, such as a hinge; a deep one holds a tenon, forming a mortise-and-tenon joint.

MULLION: A slender vertical bar separating adjoining windows; sometimes also applied to vertical dividers between the individual panes of a single window. The original Latin word meant "in the middle." See "Muntin" below.

MUNTIN: A narrow vertical or horizontal strip separating the panes of a window.

PARTING STRIP: A narrow piece of molding along the inner top and sides of the frame of a double-hung window, separating the upper and lower sashes.

RABBET: A step cut in the edge of a board, to form a joint with another board similarly cut or to hold in place thin sheet material, such as glass. The cut is called a rebate in Great Britain and Canada. Both words come from the Old French, *rabattre,* meaning to beat down or deduct.

RAIL: The horizontal top or bottom piece of a door or a window sash.

ROUGH FRAME: The framework, usually of heavy boards, surrounding a door or window opening and covered by trim.

SASH: The movable part of any window, or the frame that holds the glass; from the French *chassis,* meaning "framework." As the word evolved in English, its pronunciation changed from *shasses* to *shases* to *sashes* to *sash.*

SHIM: A thin, usually wedge-shaped piece inserted under or between other pieces to adjust their position.

SILL: The horizontal piece at the bottom of a window frame, generally slanted down toward the outside of the house to shed water. The inside, shelflike piece commonly mislabeled the sill is properly called the stool.

STILE: A vertical side piece of a door or a window sash; from the Dutch *stijl,* meaning "doorpost."

STOOL: The horizontal piece of inside trim at the base of a window, resting on the sill and projecting into the room.

STOP: A narrow strip of trim along the face of a door or window jamb, which prevents a door or a casement window from swinging too far and creates channels for double-hung window sashes.

THRESHOLD: A strip fastened to the floor beneath a door; a doorsill. The word derives from the original meaning of *thresh,* "to trample or tread."

# Simple Carpentry for Everyday Door Problems

Few working parts of a house cause more frustration than a door that rattles, sticks or refuses to lock, or even to close at all. Each problem has a number of possible causes, some obvious, some obscure. The repairs are much the same for wooden and metal doors—although wooden doors, like the ones shown on these pages, are more common. Most repairs call for no special tools or skills, but some fitting of sticky doors requires planing. There are two types of plane *(opposite)*—one for long edges, the other for short edges and for pieces that cannot be clamped in place. Both types of plane are easier to use if you understand certain techniques and know how to adjust the blade, which is called the iron.

One of the easiest of all repairs will cure a rattling door. Simply install foam-edged weather stripping against the edges of the doorstops or pull the stop from the jamb *(page 28)* and renail it closer to the closed door.

A sagging or sticking door calls for a more careful diagnosis. First, check the hinges; the screws that anchor the hinge leaves to the jamb may have pulled loose. If the screws turn but will not tighten, the screw holes in the jambs have become enlarged. In that case, fill the holes with wooden plugs and replace the screws *(page 23, top left)*.

When a door sticks even though the hinge screws are fastened securely, the problem may lie in a faulty installation of the hinges themselves. For a door to open and close freely, the hinge leaves must be recessed, or mortised, to equal depths—preferably flush with the surrounding wood.

A door that binds along the side jamb at the top of the lock side may have its bottom hinge recessed too deeply in the jamb. An easy remedy is to shim the hinge out with cardboard *(page 23, top right)*. If the clearance between the door and the jamb on the lock side is so small that you cannot shim the bottom hinge, cut a deeper mortise for the top hinge

*(page 118, Step 6)*. Similarly, for a door that binds toward the bottom of the lock side, you can either shim the upper hinge or recess the lower one more deeply.

Generally, however, it is better to avoid deepening a mortise. When the edge of the hinge leaf closest to the hinge pin has been recessed too deeply, a door may resist closing or may swing open when it is not locked. To solve this problem, insert a narrow cardboard shim behind the hinge leaf near the pin.

Paint build-up, too, can prevent a door from moving freely. One symptom of build-up is rounded corners on a door or rounded joints between the stops and the jamb. To pinpoint trouble spots, insert thin cardboard along the joint between the closed door and the jamb. Wherever the door pinches or presses the cardboard, remove the paint with a wood chisel and sandpaper as you would for a sticking window *(page 10, top left)*.

Paradoxically, sticking can also be caused by a lack of paint. A door should be sealed by paint or varnish on all of its six sides because unfinished wood absorbs moisture and expands in hot, humid weather. Correct this problem by sealing the exposed surfaces during the next cool, dry spell.

More serious is a warped door. If the door, like most interior doors, has two hinges, move the stop molding or the strike plate to accommodate the warp and then install a third hinge. A warped exterior door is usually beyond repair and must be replaced.

On a door that moves freely but will not stay closed, check to be sure that the bolt enters the opening in the strike plate when the door is shut. If the bolt and the strike-plate opening are out of alignment, you may be able to file the strike plate *(page 23, bottom)* rather than move it. If the door hits the stops before the bolt catches in the strike plate, reposition the stops farther from the closed door.

Another simple repair is a patch in a hollow-core door; all you need to fill a

hole is spackling compound and a piece of window screening *(page 26, bottom)*. Afterward, however, you must take special care not to exert pressure against the patch. Before attempting to fix a dent in a metal door, write the manufacturer for instructions; the basic repair method for most metal doors is to sand the dented area down to bare metal, then bring the dent to the level of the surrounding area with automobile-body filler.

Repairing a bowed jamb is a more complicated matter. Try to straighten a jamb that bows toward the door by the method shown on pages 24 and 25. A jamb that bows in the opposite direction must be pried away from the jack stud and straightened with shim shingles (available at most lumberyards) driven between the jamb and the stud. Do not try to straighten a bow of more than ½ inch; a jamb so deformed should be replaced. As an alternative, however, you can plane the door to fit the space.

A plane is, in fact, a versatile tool for many door repairs and installation procedures. Use a 14-inch jack plane, which is held in both hands, for planing the long edge of a door. You can also use it for beveling the edges of swinging doors *(page 124)* and for trimming shutters. To plane a door on its hinges or to work on end grains, use a block plane, which is generally about 6 inches long and light enough to be held in one hand while the other hand steadies the work.

When planing, work with the grain and remove the wood in several thin shavings. Apply pressure to the toe, or front, of the plane at the beginning of each stroke, then gradually shift the pressure to the heel, or back, as you finish the cut. For smooth cutting, lubricate the bottom of the plane, called the sole, with wax.

To protect the plane iron, always place the plane on its side when the iron is exposed; after the job is completed, retract the iron completely. When the cutting edge becomes dull or nicked, take the iron to a professional sharpener.

# How to Use a Plane

**Anatomy of a jack plane.** The iron and cap iron of a jack plane are fastened together with a cap screw to form a double iron, which rests on a slanting piece called the frog. The lever cap and its cam fasten the double iron in place; locking pressure is adjusted by turning the lever-cap screw. On the sole of the plane, the mouth opening through which the iron projects is adjusted by loosening two frog-bed screws and turning a frog-adjusting screw; move the frog forward for fine work, back for coarse planing.

The cap iron, which acts as a chip breaker, may also be adjusted. Set it about 1/16 inch behind the cutting edge of the iron for all-purpose planing; move it closer for fine jobs. The adjusting nut controls the depth of the cut the iron makes, and the adjusting lever aligns the iron's cutting edge. A knob and a handle mounted on the sole provide holds for two hands.

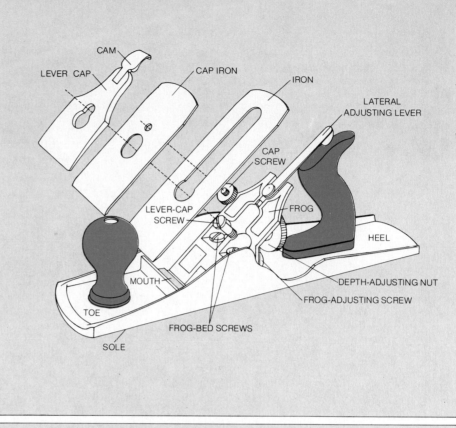

**Anatomy of a block plane.** The single iron of a block plane lies at a lower angle than the iron of a jack plane, and the bevel of the iron faces up rather than down. The lever-cap screw and the locking lever tighten the lever cap directly against the iron; a second lever, secured by a finger rest on the toe of the plane, adjusts the mouth opening. An adjusting nut controls the depth of the cut, and a third lever aligns the cutting edge laterally. On this small plane the vertical flanges, called wings, provide a handhold for one-handed operation.

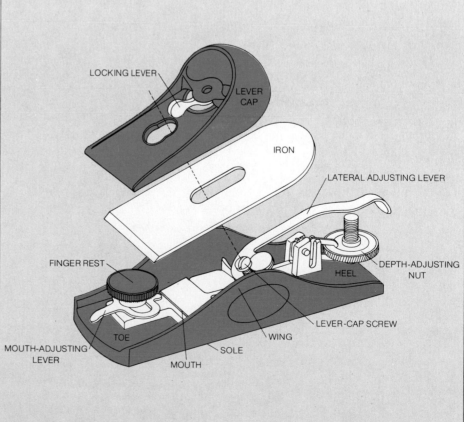

**Adjusting the plane iron.** Hold the plane—in this example, a jack plane—upside down over a light-colored background and sight along the sole. Turn the adjusting nut until the edge of the iron is visible at the mouth opening, then use the nut to bring the iron to the desired depth of cut; the final turn of the nut should always move the iron outward. If the iron projects unevenly across the width of the mouth, move the adjusting lever to correct its alignment (*inset*).

**Using a jack plane.** Secure the board to be planed in a vise so that you can cut with the grain, and set a jack plane squarely on the edge (*below*). Grip the handle of the plane with one hand and hold the thumb of the other against the knob, curling the remaining fingers of this hand under the sole and against the face of the board as a guide for a straight cut—provided the wood is smooth; otherwise grip the knob. After a few strokes of the plane, lay a long, straight piece of scrap lumber on the planed surface and mark any high points for further planing. As a final check for squareness, slide a combination square along the full length of the angle formed by the face and edge of the board, and mark and plane any remaining high points.

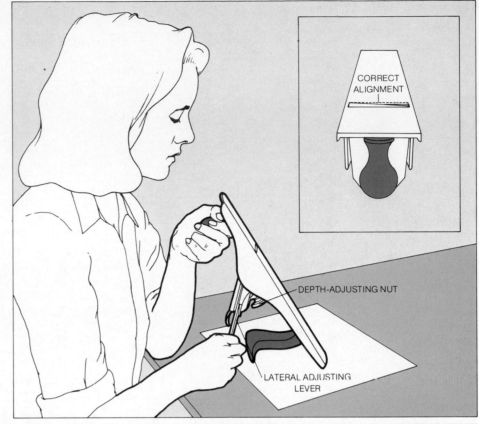

CORRECT ALIGNMENT

DEPTH-ADJUSTING NUT

LATERAL ADJUSTING LEVER

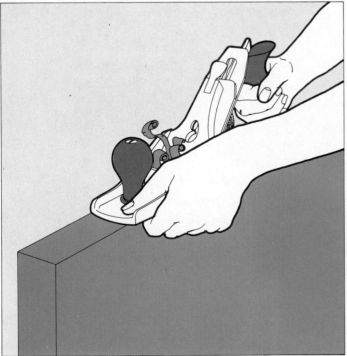

**Using a block plane.** Mark the parts of the edge to be trimmed and adjust a block plane for a fine cut. With the board steadied with one hand, hold the plane by its wings in your other hand, set your index finger on the finger rest and plane the marked areas.

## Resetting Hinges and Plates

**Tightening loose screws.** Remove the door and the hinge. Cut lengths of dowel or whittle wooden plugs to the size of the hinge-screw holes, coat the plugs with glue and tap them into the holes. Let the glue set for at least an hour, then drill pilot holes through the plugs and screw the hinges back in place.

**Shimming a hinge.** Wedge the door open, loosen the screws that fasten a hinge leaf to the jamb and insert a cardboard shim, slotted at the level of the screws, behind the hinge leaf. Add a second shim if necessary.

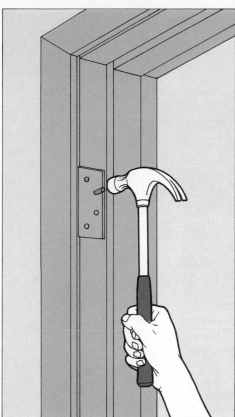

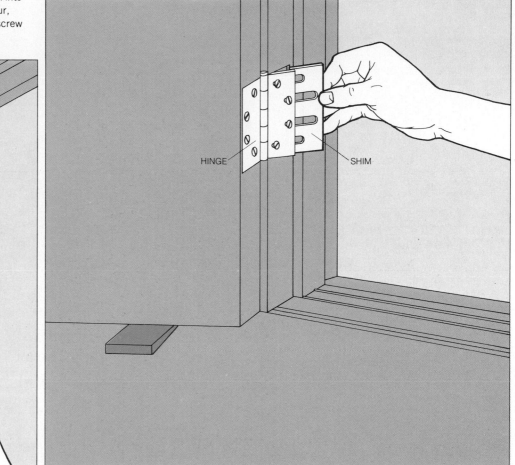

HINGE          SHIM

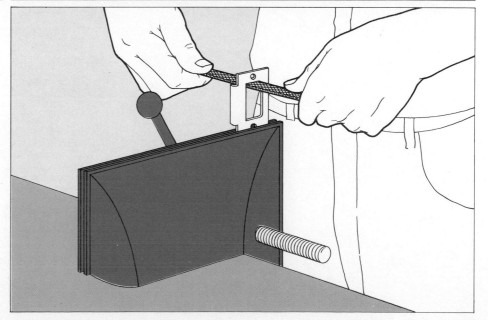

**Filing a strike plate.** If an ordinary strike plate is less than ¼ inch out of alignment with the bolt (for a larger misalignment, see page 123, Step 3), enlarge the plate opening with a flat double-cut file. Remove $1/16$ inch of metal at a time until the bolt fits. Enlarge the strike-plate hole in the jamb with a chisel if necessary.

## Shaving a Door to Fit

**Trimming the edges.** If a door sticks at the top, wedge it halfway open and use a block plane to trim the top. Plane from the sides of the door toward the center until there is ⅛ inch of clearance at the head jamb.

If a door sticks all along a long edge, take the door off the hinges—drive the pins up and out, bottom hinge first, then the middle, and finally the top hinge. Remove the hinges and support the door with a door jack (*page 121*) or have a helper hold it on edge; trim the hinge-side edge with a jack plane; deepen the hinge mortises if necessary before replacing the hinges.

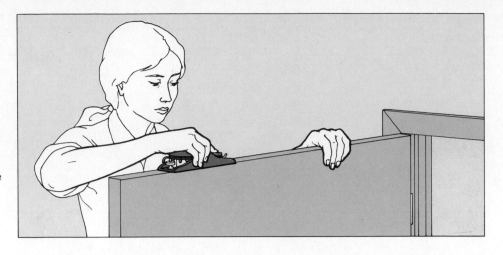

## Straightening a Jamb

**1** **Marking the bow.** Wedge the door open, set a long, straight scrap of plywood against the jamb and mark the high point of the bow. For an exterior door, remove only the casing that is inside the house (*page 28*). For an interior door, remove the casing on both sides of the partition.

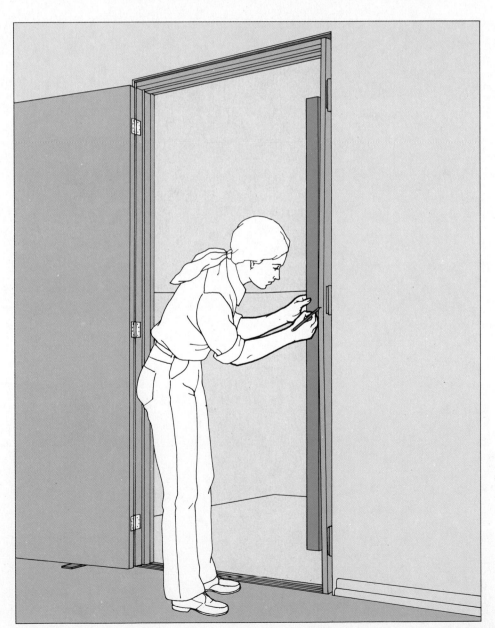

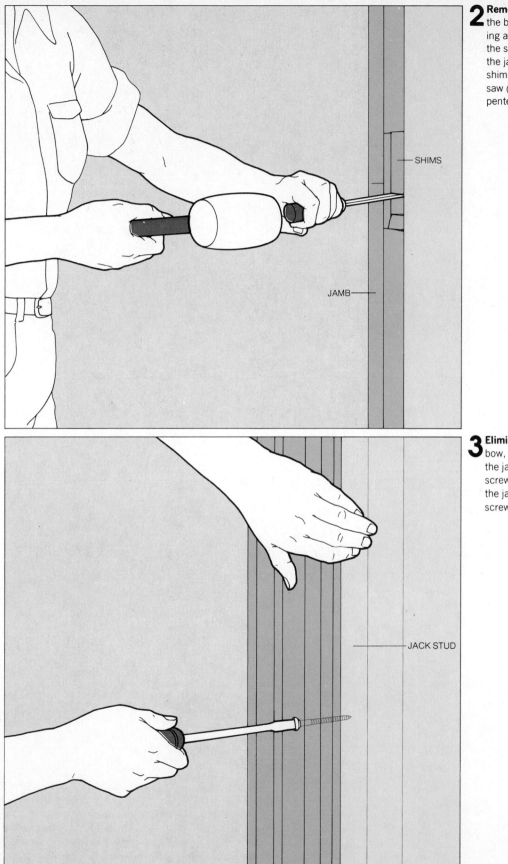

SHIMS

JAMB

JACK STUD

**2** **Removing the shims.** Pry the entire length of the bowed jamb away from the jack stud and, using a mallet and a ¼-inch wood chisel, split the shims that are nailed between the jamb and the jack stud and pull out the fragments. If the shims do not split easily, cut the nails with a hacksaw *(page 34, Step 3)* or pull them with carpenter's nippers *(page 28)*.

**3** **Eliminating the bow.** At the high point of the bow, use a counterbore bit to drill a hole through the jamb for a 2½-inch No. 12 flathead wood screw. Drive the screw through the high point of the jamb and into the jack stud, tightening the screw until the jamb is vertical.

**4** **Reshimming the jamb.** On an exterior door, insert the butt end of a shim between the jamb and the jack stud just below the screw used to straighten the jamb. Cut 3 inches from the thin end of a second shim and tap this end into the opening alongside the first shim. Drive two 16-penny finishing nails through the jamb and shims into the jack stud. Install a pair of shims at the level of each of the shims on the other side of the door, and add two more pairs in the unshimmed spaces.

On an interior door, insert full-sized shims, thin end first, from opposite sides of the jamb, nail them, then score and break off their ends.

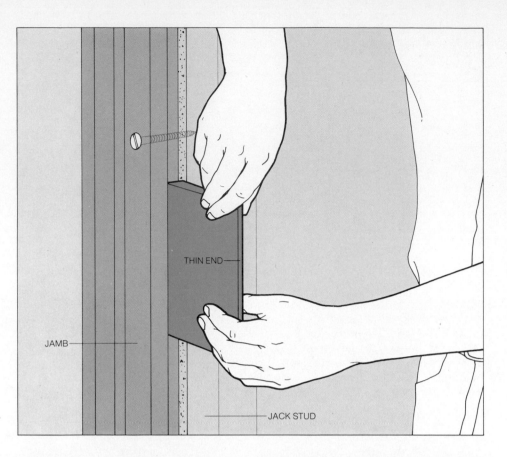

## Patching a Hollow-Core Door

**Filling the hole.** Loop a cord through a piece of wire screening slightly larger than the hole, moisten the area around the hole, then insert the screening in the hole and pull it flush to the inside of the door. Holding the cord taut, spread spackling compound around the edges of the hole, working gradually toward the center. To hold the screening while the compound dries, tie the cord to a dowel or pencil long enough to bridge the patch, and turn the dowel until it fits snugly against the face of the door (inset).

When the patch dries, remove the dowel, cut the cord flush to the surface of the patch, and lightly sand the first layer. Apply a second coat of compound, allow this layer to dry, then sand the patch to a smooth finish.

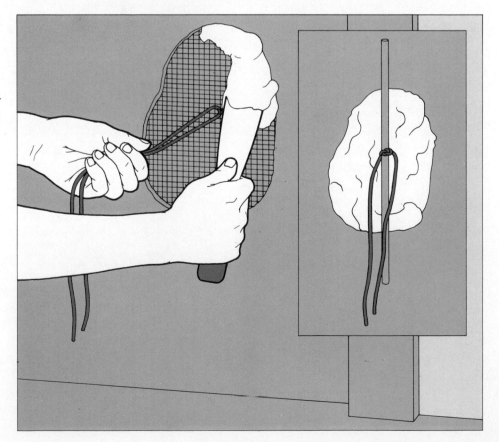

# Repairs for a Sliding Door

Like hinged doors, sliding glass units sometimes bind or jam completely—but for different reasons. The track in which the door glides may be dirty or dented, the rollers beneath it worn or broken.

Removing debris trapped in a track is simple enough: use a stiff brush and a vacuum cleaner. But to mend a dented track or replace broken rollers you must remove the door. You may have to lower it by turning roller-adjusting screws located on the face of the door (page 106, Step 7) or, as in the metal door shown here, on the edge. Lift the door out of the track and tilt it out of the opening.

For metal doors, remove the bottom rail (right, Step 1) to get at the roller units, since rail and rollers are generally held in place by the same screws. Roller units for wooden doors can usually be replaced without removing the rail.

On both types, a slightly dented track can be easily and inexpensively fitted with a snap-on stainless-steel channel (below, right); a mashed track must be replaced. When replacing a track or roller, you must match the original part exactly; you may have to write the door manufacturer for the name of a supplier.

## Replacing the Rollers

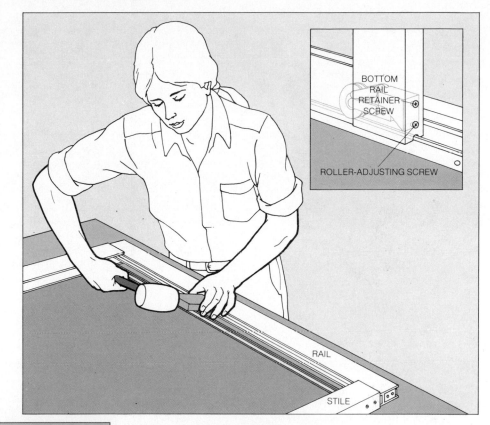

**1** **Removing the bottom rail.** Lay the door on a flat surface, remove the bottom-rail retainer screws (inset) and, while a helper holds the door steady, tap a wood block against the top of the rail to free the rail from the door.

BOTTOM RAIL RETAINER SCREW

ROLLER-ADJUSTING SCREW

RAIL

STILE

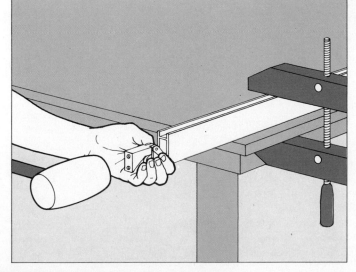

**2** **Installing the rollers.** Clamp the bottom rail to a table and slide the worn or broken roller units out of the rail, prying with a screwdriver if necessary. Tap new units into each end of the rail, with the rollers facing the middle of the door.

## A New Channel for an Old Track

**Installing the track channel.** With a hacksaw, cut a stainless-steel channel to the length of the dented track, then snap the channel onto the old track, pressing it down with a wood block. Readjust the rollers (page 106, Step 7).

# Remedies of Last Resort: Working on the Trim

Trim for a door or window is more than decoration. The stops—the strips of trim inside the top and sides of the opening—keep a door or the sash of a casement window from swinging too far and help to seal the gaps between the door or window and the jambs that enclose it on three sides. On a window with sliding sashes—a double-hung window for example—the stops define the channels in which the sashes move.

The interior sill of a window, called the stool, acts as a kind of bottom stop; the exterior sill, called the finish sill, is angled to carry water away from the window, and also forms the base of the window frame, like a bottom jamb. Even the molded interior casing does useful work: it strengthens the framework of jambs, hides the gaps between the jambs and the wall and conceals the shims that level the door or the window.

The following pages explain how to remove old trim and install new; though

the illustrations show the trim work on a door, the instructions apply to both doors and windows.

Lumberyards carry trim pieces in a variety of shapes, thicknesses and widths, but to match the trim of an old house, you will have to check secondhand building-supply yards. Otherwise you can have the piece cut specially—and expensively—at a mill; this custom work may entail the shaping of a special blade to cut your pattern.

The casing is one of the most carefully fitted elements of the trim. Its position depends on the type of unit it surrounds. On doors and casement windows, the casing is conventionally set back ⅛ inch from the inside edge of the jamb. On double-hung windows, the casing is generally set flush with the inside edge of the jamb, forming a three-part joint with the interior stop.

Where pieces of casing meet, the joints are generally mitered. The top piece has

two 45° miter cuts, fitting similar cuts at the tops of the side pieces to form right angles. Some windows are cased like picture frames, with four casing strips miter-cut to 45° angles at the ends.

Stops, like casing, may be mitered. On molded stops, however, the professional technique is to cope the side stops to fit the contour of the head stop (page 32, Step 2), making a joint that will not separate as easily as a mitered one.

Both casing and stops should be nailed with special care. Drive each nail until the nailhead alone projects above the wood surface, then complete the job with a nail set. Be sure never to drive the nail in at a sharp slant—by doing so you can pull the jamb out of alignment. On a double-hung window with sash pulleys and weight pockets (page 12), be careful not to drive the nails into the pocket. And when nailing door casing, do not drive a nail at the location of a strike plate (page 123).

## Removing Casing and Stops

**Pulling out the stops.** Score the joints between the stop and the jamb with a utility knife, then, starting at the bottom of a side stop, set a ¾-inch chisel between stop and jamb, with the bevel of the chisel against the jamb. Tapping the chisel with a mallet, work up the stop to pry it away from the jamb. Repeat the procedure on the other side stop, then on the head stop.

**Prying off the casing.** Take the casing partway off with a chisel, as for a stop, then insert the flat end of a pry bar behind the outer edge of the casing. Place a thin scrap of wood behind the bar to avoid marring the wall. Slowly pry the casing completely free, working up from the bottom of the side casing. Remove the other side casing and the head casing in the same way.

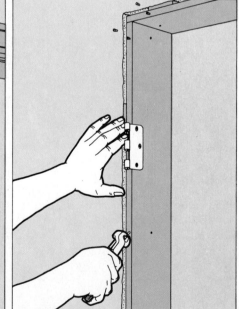

**Extracting nails.** If a finishing nail does not come out with the casing but remains embedded in the jamb or wall, grip the head with carpenter's nippers and roll the nipper head against the wall to twist the nail free. If the nail is in a stop or casing that you plan to reuse, grip the shank of the nail protruding at the back and pull the head end completely through the piece.

# Cutting New Casing

**1 Measuring the head casing.** For doors and casement windows, use a combination square to mark at several points the conventional setback of the casing, ⅛ inch outside the inner edge of the jambs; the marks for the top and side pieces of casing should intersect at a precise corner point. On most double-hung windows, you need not make these marks, because the casing is positioned flush with the inside of the jambs.

Measure the distance between the side jambs at the top; for doors and casement windows, add ¼ inch to allow for the setbacks at the sides. Mark this distance on the edge of a piece of casing that is long enough to leave room for the miter cuts, which will fan outward from the marks.

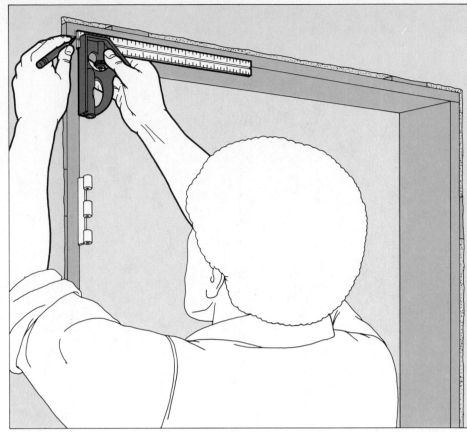

**2 Cutting the miters.** In a miter box bolted to a workbench, place the casing flat side down, set the saw for a 45° cut outward from the mark and, using long, even strokes, saw the strip just outside one of the marks you have made. Reverse the 45° angle and cut the second miter just outside the mark at the other end.

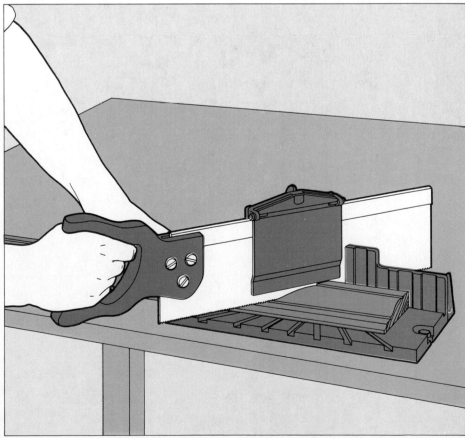

**3** **Coping the backs of the miters.** To make the joints fit smoothly, cope a crescent-shaped piece from the back of each mitered end of the top casing strip. Leave an uncoped ½-inch margin at the top and bottom edges of the strip.

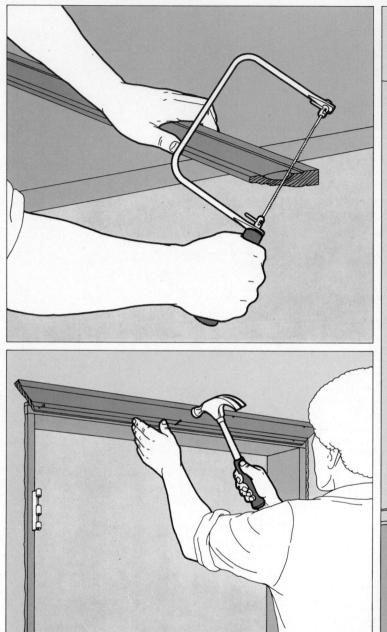

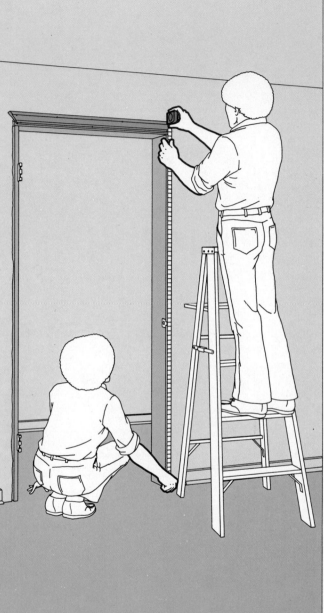

**4** **Nailing the top casing.** With a helper, set the narrow edge of the casing at the corners of the jambs of double-hung windows or at the marks on the jambs of doors and casement windows, then tack the ends of the casing to the head jamb. Starting from one end, drive fourpenny finishing nails through the bottom of the casing into the jamb and sixpenny finishing nails along the outer edge of the casing into the header, spacing the nails at least 12 inches apart. Set the nails and spackle the holes.

**5** **Measuring the side pieces.** For a door, measure the distance from the bottom of a miter in the top casing to the floor; for a window, measure to the stool. Add ¹⁄₁₆ inch to this and mark the total length on the narrow edge of a casing strip that is long enough to allow for an outward miter at one end. Square off the strip at one mark and make a 45° outward cut from the other (*page 29, Step 2*). Stand the side casing in place to check the fit of the miter; plane the side miter with a block plane if necessary. Similarly mark, cut and fit the other side casing.

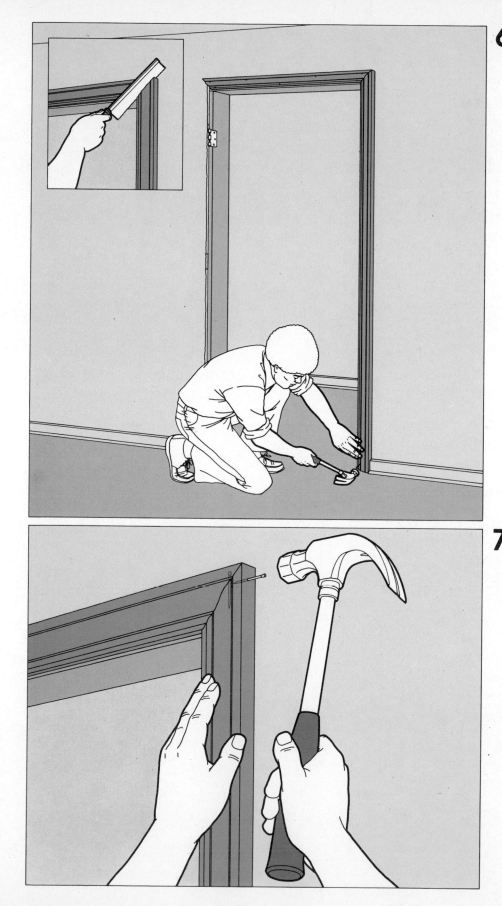

**6 Attaching the side pieces.** With the mitered joint aligned, tack the side casing in position—⅛ inch from the inner edge of the side jamb on a door or a casement window, flush with the jamb edge on a double-hung window. Starting at the top, nail the casing to the jamb and the studs, using fourpenny finishing nails at the jamb, six-penny at the studs. If there is an uneven gap in a miter joint after the casing is nailed in place, you can improve the fit by cutting through the joint with a dovetail saw *(inset)*; the casing pieces are so flexible that lock-nailing *(Step 7, below)* will close the kerf left by the saw.

**7 Lock-nailing the joints.** An inch from the outside corner of the casing, drive one fourpenny finishing nail vertically down through the top edge of the top casing into the side casing, and another horizontally through the edge of the side casing and into the top casing. The joint should now be even and tight.

# Adding New Stops

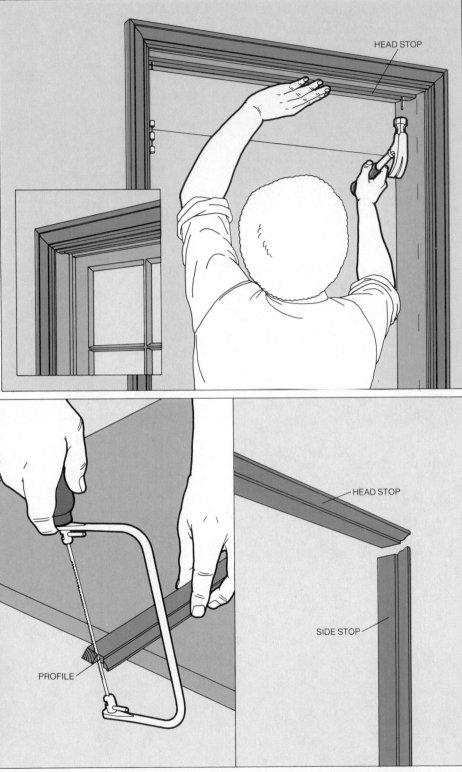

**1** **Positioning the head stop.** Cut stop molding to fit between the tops of the side jambs and nail it in place temporarily. Its position depends on the fixture you are trimming. For a door or a casement window, set the square edge of the stop against the closed door or sash. If the door or window has been removed or has not yet been hung, as in the drawing at right, note the direction in which it will swing and, starting from that side of the opening, mark the thickness of the door or sash on the head and side jambs and set the square edge of the stop at the marks.

For a double-hung window, the head stop fits against the closed sash and generally fills the space between the sash channel and the inside edge of the head jamb (*inset*). On double-hung windows that slide in tracks (*page 14*), set the stops against the raised edges of the tracks.

HEAD STOP

HEAD STOP

SIDE STOP

MITER

PROFILE

**2** **Coping the side stops.** For a door, cut two lengths of stop stock an inch longer than the distance from the head jamb to the floor; for a window, measure to the stool. Flat stops can be butted together; for mitered stops, cut a 45° miter across the molded face at the top end of each piece, angling from the molded face to the flat face that fits against the jamb (*left*). The cuts will leave a scalloped profile on each molded face. Trace the profiles with a pencil and, following the marks, make a 90° cut through each piece with a coping saw (*center*). The ends of the coped pieces will fit snugly against the head stop (*right*). Measure the lengths of the side stops, trim them at the bottom and nail them in place temporarily as you did the head stop.

If a door or a casement window binds or rattles against the tacked stops, move the stops for a better fit. Then secure each stop with fourpenny finishing nails 16 inches apart.

# The Base of a Window: Sill, Stool and Apron

The parts of a window most vulnerable to damage and decay are the trim pieces at the base, which are frequently bumped, banged and rained on. Each has a special name *(top, right)* that can be confusing because the terminology is often mixed up in common usage. The finish sill, for example, is exposed outdoors only; the indoor "sill" is properly called a stool.

The finish sill is usually the first piece to show signs of wear. If it is merely cracked or pitted, try to restore rather than replace it. Remove all the paint, splinters and wood chips, using paint remover, putty knife and wire brush, then coat the sill with wood preservative. Let it dry for a day and give it two coats of linseed oil, allowing a day for drying after each application. Fill cracks and holes with putty, let the putty dry for a couple of days, then prime and repaint the sill.

A rotted finish sill has to be replaced, however, and promptly, to prevent the spread of rot to the rest of the window. You should be able to match your sill at a local lumberyard; if not, you will have to order the lumber specially milled, for it must fit exactly into dadoes, or grooves, in the side jambs *(top, inset)*. When buying a new sill, get one with a drip groove under the outside edge to prevent water from creeping up the bottom of the sill, and with an angle cut along the inside edge to make this edge vertical when the sill is in place.

Some older windows, assembled on the job, do not have dadoes in the side jambs to hold the finish sill. In their place, you may find an intricate pattern of sill-to-jamb joinery almost impossible for an amateur to duplicate. If you do, have a professional replace the sill or—probably at lower cost—replace the entire window *(pages 76-78)*.

Replacing a stool calls for a new piece that will fit your sill and walls—and these may vary from the modern standard. If your window needs a stool wider than the standard stock, either adapt the stock by gluing and tacking a strip of wood to the edge that fits against the window sash, or order a specially milled stool.

**The trim at the base of a window.** In a double-hung window, a finish sill fits into side jambs seated in dadoes *(inset)* that slope down outward 15° for drainage. Outside, the sill rests on a horizontal 2-by-4—the rough sill. Extensions of the finish sill, sill horns, fit against the outside edges of the jambs, providing a base for the exterior casing, or brickmold *(not shown)*. These horns vary in length, but need extend no farther than the outer edges of the brickmold. Inside the house, a stool fits over the finish sill, with stool horns generally extending ¾ inch beyond the edges of the interior casing. The bottom of the stool has a beveled rabbet that is angled to set it firmly on the sloping sill. An apron under the stool conceals the gap between the finish sill and the rough sill beneath it, and adds support to the stool.

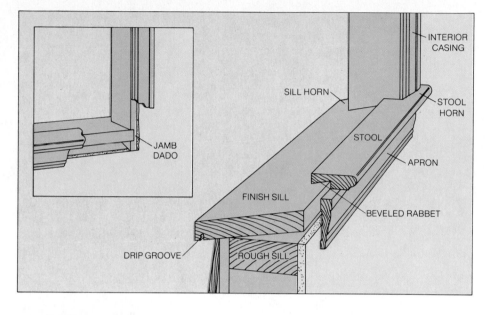

JAMB DADO

INTERIOR CASING

SILL HORN

STOOL HORN

STOOL

APRON

BEVELED RABBET

FINISH SILL

DRIP GROOVE

ROUGH SILL

## Getting At the Sill

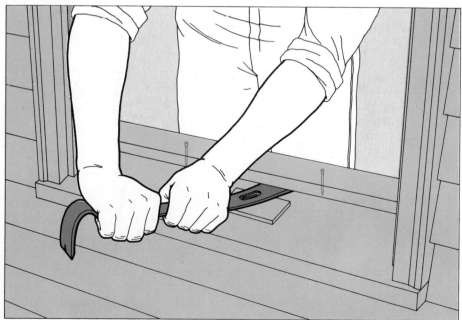

**1 Removing the stool.** Take off the interior side casings and stops *(page 28)*, pry off the apron with a chisel and pry bar, and raise the bottom sash. If you plan to replace the stool, simply hit the stool from underneath with a hammer, but if you wish to reuse the stool, you must pry it off from outside *(above)* after several preliminary steps. First check to see if the stool has been nailed to the studs through the horns; if so, drive the nails completely through the stool with a blunted nail. Then lean out the window, ease a pry bar between the stool and the sill, set a scrap of wood under the bar and gently pry the stool off.

**2 Removing the finish sill.** Measure and make a notation of the exact distance between the side jambs, then make two cuts approximately a foot apart through the middle of the sill with a crosscut saw. Pry off the cut section and pull the end pieces out of their dadoes *(inset);* if you cannot free the end pieces easily, pry the bottom of the brickmold on each side slightly away from the wall. Caution: work slowly and carefully in order to avoid racking or splitting the jambs.

If the jambs have moved inward, use a hammer and a block of wood to tap them back to their original position. If there are no shims behind the jambs at dado level, install shims to prevent the jambs from moving too far apart.

**3 Removing the nails.** Working inside the house with a hacksaw blade, cut off the exposed parts of the nails that secured the sill inside the dadoes. The blade can be held in a gloved hand, but the job will go faster with an inexpensive blade holder like the one pictured.

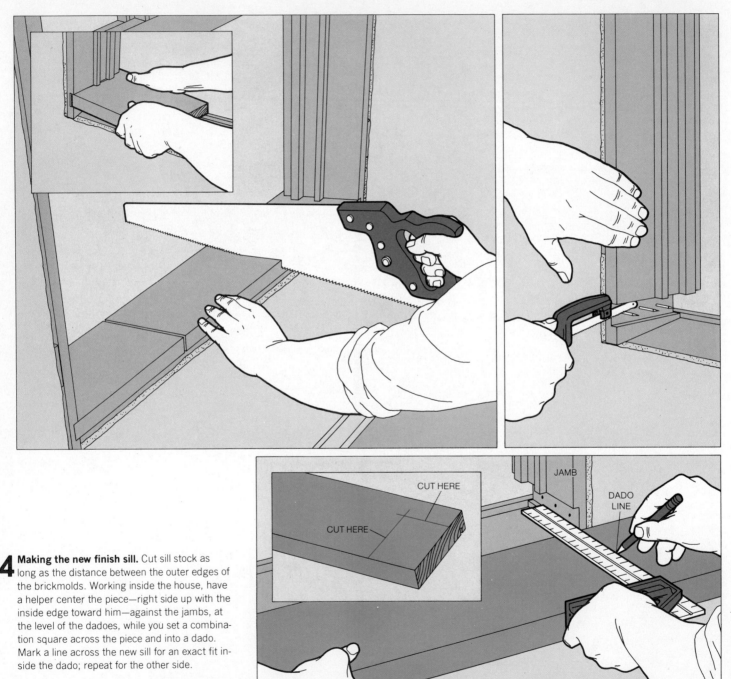

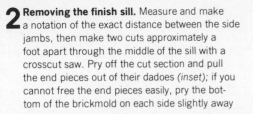

**4 Making the new finish sill.** Cut sill stock as long as the distance between the outer edges of the brickmolds. Working inside the house, have a helper center the piece—right side up with the inside edge toward him—against the jambs, at the level of the dadoes, while you set a combination square across the piece and into a dado. Mark a line across the new sill for an exact fit inside the dado; repeat for the other side.

On the lines you have drawn, mark off the length of the dado, measuring from the inside edge of the sill. Draw perpendicular lines from these marks to the ends of the sill *(inset)*. Cut out the inside corners to fit the dadoes and leave sill horns; saw on the waste side of the lines.

**5** **Installing the sill.** Push the inside corners of the sill 1 or 2 inches into the dadoes in the jambs, then set a piece of scrap wood against the outside edge of the sill and tap lightly with a hammer until the inside edge of the sill is flush with the inside edges of the jambs.

Inside the house, drill pilot holes angling through the inside edge of the sill into the side jambs and toenail the sill in place with eightpenny nails *(inset)*. Outside the house, drill pilot holes straight through from the front edge of the sill horns into the studs of the rough frame; secure with nails. Caulk all exterior joints.

## Fitting a Stool and Apron

**1** **Marking the stool.** Measure the distance between the outer edges of the interior casings (their positions will be visible on the wall even after you have removed the casings) and add 1½ inches; measure the depth of the window from the inside edge of the jamb to the far edge of the interior stop and add the thickness of the interior casing plus ¾ inch. Cut stool stock to this total length and width. With a helper centering the stool piece—right side up, inner, molded edge toward him—against the jambs, level with the finish sill, set the blade of a combination square across the piece and against the inner face of each side jamb; draw lines from the jamb faces across the stool. Extend these lines down across the squared, outside edge of the stool.

Starting at points directly above the inner corners of the rabbet on the stool's underside, draw lines from each end of the stool to intersect the jamb lines at a right angle *(inset)*. Cut out corners for the stool horns on the waste sides of the lines. Slip the stool into position, with its rabbet fitted to the top corner of the sill, and close the window sash. There should be a ¹⁄₁₆-inch gap between the sash and the stool; if you find too little clearance, plane the stool down and sand the planed area smooth. Finish the ends of the horns as shown at the bottom of page 36.

**2** **Attaching the stool.** At points in the corners of the stool that will be covered by the side stops, and at two additional points to the left and right of the center, drill pilot holes and drive eight-penny finishing nails down through the top of the stool into the sill. Then replace the casings and the stops *(pages 29-32).*

**3** **Installing the apron.** Cut a piece of apron stock 1½ inches shorter than the stool, finish the ends *(bottom of page)* and set it in place, centered under the stool. Fasten the apron with three sixpenny nails along the top—one at the center and one at each end—and three fourpenny nails similarly spaced along the bottom.

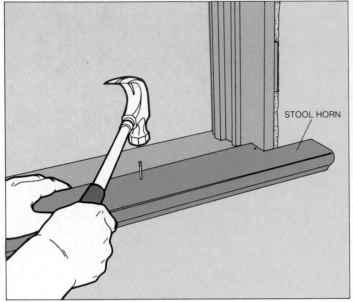

STOOL HORN

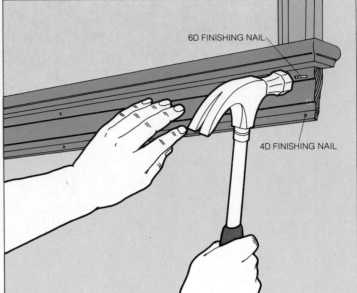

6D FINISHING NAIL

4D FINISHING NAIL

## Three Ways of Shaping the Ends

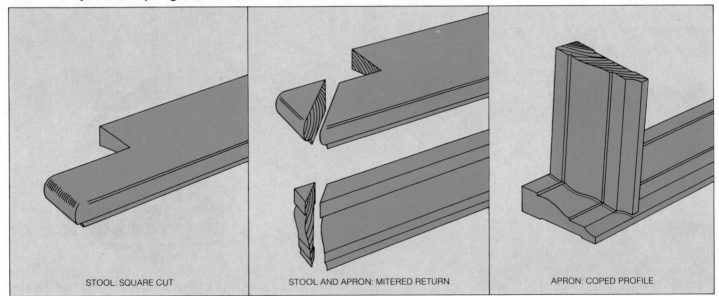

STOOL: SQUARE CUT

STOOL AND APRON: MITERED RETURN

APRON: COPED PROFILE

**Rounded, mitered and coped.** You can, of course, simply square the ends of a stool or apron with a backsaw and miter box, smooth the cuts with sandpaper, then nail the piece in place. Most professionals, however, prefer to use techniques that give the window a more finished appearance. For a stool, they may cut the ends square, then round them with a rasp and sand them smooth *(above, left).* For both a

stool and an apron, a more elaborate technique is the mitered return *(above, center).* Cut the stool or apron to length and miter the ends inward at 45°. Cut two scrap pieces of trim into triangular wedges, with a miter cut at one end to fit the mitered end of the apron and a square cut at the other end to fit against the wall, then glue and nail the wedges in place. A third finishing method, which is used for an apron with a molded

pattern on its face, is to cope the ends to the same profile as the face. Cut the apron about an inch too long at each end and mark the correct end positions on the face. Set a scrap piece of apron stock on end at the marks *(above, right)* and trace the profile of the piece; then cut the apron along the traced line with a coping saw, keeping the saw straight, and smooth the cut ends of the apron with sandpaper.

# Fine Work on Treasured Windows

A window sash in traditional style is an interlocking grid of wood holding small panes of glass. Vertical stiles and horizontal rails form the sturdy outer framework of the sash; relatively fragile strips called muntins support the panes within. All of these wooden pieces are snugly jointed with interlocking notches and projections called mortises and tenons. To preserve the beauty of a valuable or antique window, it is better to replace individual parts, when necessary, than to substitute an entire modern sash.

Replacing a muntin—the piece most likely to be damaged when a window is broken—is an especially intricate job. To replace a single vertical muntin, you must take the whole sash apart. To replace one of the shorter horizontal muntins, either dismantle the sash or use the shortcut method shown overleaf. In both methods, you must first take the sash out of the window and carefully remove all the glass *(pages 50-51)*, keeping each pane intact for reinstallation, before you can work on the muntin.

To ensure a proper fit, always get a new muntin of the same design as the one it replaces. Most window dealers stock a variety of muntin designs; if you cannot match your own, you can have one specially milled. The wooden pins that lock the muntin tenons into the mortises can be easily shaped by hand from scrap lumber; alternatively, steel pins are available from window dealers.

Not all muntins are individually fitted together. If the one you must replace is a part of a decorative one-piece grille fitted over a single pane of glass, a window dealer should be able to supply a wooden or plastic replacement. These grilles, which generally come with instructions, are simply snapped into place.

**The intricate joinery of a sash.** In this traditional window sash, the ends of horizontal rails are shaped into projections (called tenons), which fit into holes (called mortises) cut into the ends of the vertical stiles. Each of these mortise-and-tenon joints is secured by a wooden or steel pin driven completely through it. The interior wood strips, called muntins, are also joined with mortises and tenons. The tenons of the vertical muntins fit into mortises in the rails. Horizontal muntins have tenons that fit into mortises in the vertical muntins and the stiles.

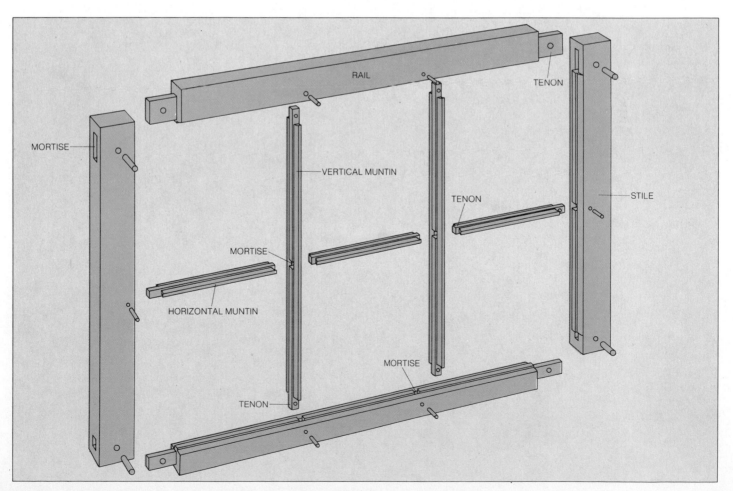

# Splicing a Short Muntin

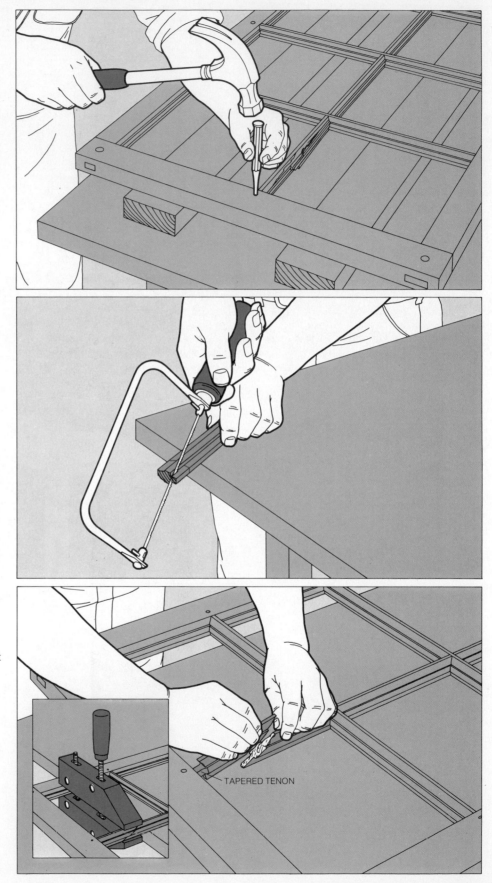

**1 Removing the pin.** Take the sash out of the window (*pages 12, 14*), remove the panes of glass (*pages 50-51*) and set the sash on scraps of wood. If the damaged muntin fits into a stile, scrape the paint and putty from the pin in the muntin's mortise-and-tenon joint, then drive the pin completely out of the hole with a center punch, a blunted nail or—best of all—a wooden dowel of the same shape and diameter as the pin. Cut the damaged muntin in half, pull its tenons out of the mortises and set the pieces aside. Cut a new muntin ⅛ inch longer than the combined length of the two pieces you have removed.

**2 Shaping the new muntin.** Judging by eye and using the old muntin as a guide, mark the shape of the tenons on the new muntin and use a coping saw to cut the ends of the new muntin to the desired shape of the tenons.

**3 Fitting the new muntin.** Make a diagonal cut through the center of the new muntin and taper the ends of the tenons slightly to ease their fit; then coat the diagonal surfaces with waterproof glue, insert the tenons into the mortises, and clamp the two pieces of the muntin together for at least 12 hours (*inset*).

If the muntin is one that fits into a stile, drill through the pinholes of the stile to make a hole in the new tenon. Coat a pin with glue and gently tap it into place with a mallet.

TAPERED TENON

## Replacing a Long Muntin

**1** **Dismantling the sash.** Take the sash out of the window, remove the glass and knock out all pins (*Step 1, opposite*). Have a helper hold the rails fast, and use a rubber mallet to tap off the stiles. Work the rails free of the muntins, then pull the tenons of the horizontal muntins out of the mortises in the vertical muntins.

**2** **Making a new vertical muntin.** Using the damaged muntin as a guide, mark a length of muntin stock for the mortise, tenon and end cuts, and cut the stock to length. Clamp the muntin to a scrap of wood on a workbench, drill holes through the muntin within the lines of each marked mortise, then pare out square mortises with a chisel. Shape tapered tenons at the ends of the muntin (*opposite, Step 2*).

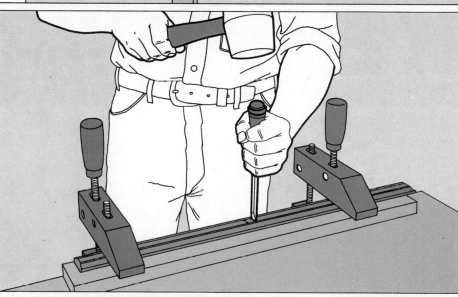

**3** **Reassembling the sash.** Fit all the muntins together and insert the tenons of the vertical muntins into the mortises of the rails; then, holding the outer horizontal muntins in place, slide the mortises of the stiles onto the tenons of the rails and horizontal muntins. Drive the pieces together with light blows of a mallet. Drill through all pinholes in the rails and stiles and gently tap pins into place.

# Prescriptions for Screens, Blinds and Shutters

Screens, blinds, shades and shutters help control air and light, and can improve the appearance of a house. They also wear out and must be repaired or replaced.

Each of the two most common screening materials, aluminum and fiberglass, has its pattern of resistance to damage. Aluminum is less likely to tear or sag; fiberglass will not corrode or oxidize. Whatever your screens are made of, match the repair method to the nature and extent of the damage. Oxidized or dirt-encrusted aluminum screening, for example, needs only rubbing with a wire brush and a once-over with a vacuum cleaner to restore it to its original condition. Loose joints on wooden frames can easily be reinforced with corrugated fasteners, angle plates or screws.

Holes in screening can be fixed in several ways. Fixing a very small hole may mean simply pushing the wires of the screening back into line with the tip of an awl. Other small gaps can be plugged with dabs of weatherproof glue or with patches glued in place. On metal screening you can also fasten patches by weaving the wires at the edges of the patch into the surrounding mesh, or you can use ready-made patches with edging wires prehooked to clip onto the screening. On fiberglass screening, iron patches in place: simply set a fiberglass patch over the hole, cover the patch with a cotton rag and run a hot iron over the rag, fusing the patch to the screening.

If the holes are so large that you cannot patch them, or so close to the frame that the screening sags, replace the screening completely. The method of re-placement depends on the type of frame. On all metal frames and some wooden ones, screening is secured with a spline—a thin strip pressed down over the screening and into a channel at the inside edges of the frame. To replace the screening, you must pull out the old spline and screening, then put the spline (a new spline if the old one is broken or brittle) back in place over new screening. The only specialized tool you will need is a simple one—a screen-spline roller.

On some wooden frames the screening is secured with tacks or staples that normally are concealed by molding. Professionals install new screening while the frame is slightly bowed by clamps (*page 42, Step 2*); when the clamps are released, the frame itself tightens the screening as it straightens out.

## A Spline for Screening on a Channeled Frame

SPLINE CHANNEL    CONVEX WHEEL    SCREEN-SPLINE ROLLER    CONCAVE WHEEL    SPLINE

**1** **Securing a short side.** Cut a piece of screening to the outer dimensions of the frame. If your screening is metal, crease it into the spline channel on a short side of the frame, using the convex wheel of a screen-spline roller (*left*); start at a corner and work in short back-and-forth strokes. With the concave wheel, force the spline into the channel over the screening (*right*). Fiberglass will not crease: roll the spline down over the screening in one step. New spline must be cut off at the corners of the frame and tamped into place with a screwdriver.

**2** **Completing the splines.** Pull the screening taut at the opposite side of the frame, crease it if necessary and roll a length of spline over it and into the channel. If the frame bows inward, fit a temporary brace to hold the sides parallel. With the screening pulled flat across the frame, spline the two remaining sides.

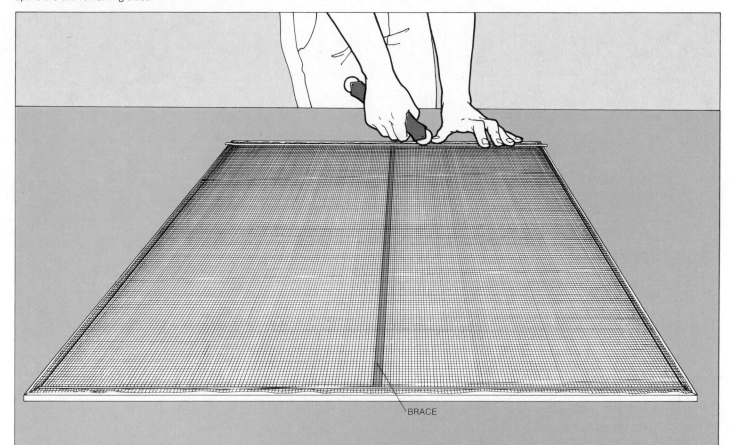

BRACE

**3** **Trimming the excess screening.** With a utility knife, cut through the screening along the outer edges of the spline channels. As you cut, slant the blade toward the outside of the frame, in order to avoid cutting into the spline.

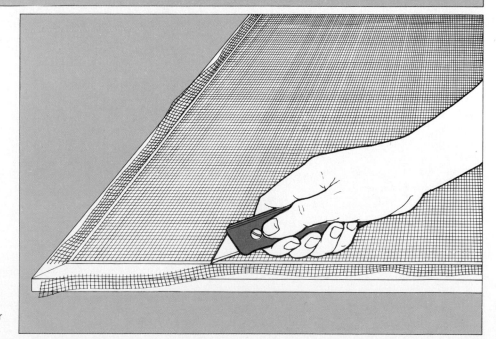

# Stapling Screening to a Wooden Frame

**1** **Fastening the first side.** Cut metal screening 2 inches larger than the frame opening. Staple the screening to a short side of the frame at 2-inch intervals, starting at a corner. Angle each staple so that its prongs fit over two different strands of the mesh. Fiberglass screening must have a hem—a double layer at the edges—to keep the screening from tearing along the line of staples. Cut the screening ½ inch larger than the outer edges of the molding that will conceal the staples. To make the hem, fold the extra ½ inch over as you staple (*inset*).

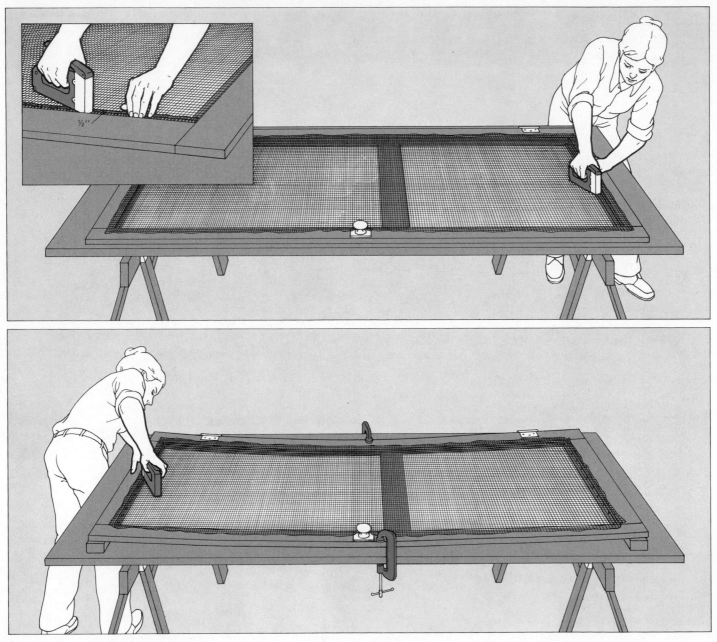

**2** **Bowing the frame.** Set blocks of scrap wood under the short sides of the frame and use a pair of C clamps to force the centers of the long sides down about ¼ inch. Pull the screening taut along the unstapled short side, staple it there and release the C clamps. Staple the long sides, replace the molding and, on metal screening, trim off the excess screening with a utility knife.

# The Anatomy of Blinds and Window Shades

A Venetian blind is a delicate affair, prone to frayed cords, torn tapes and bent or broken slats. You must dismantle the blind (below, right) to replace such parts with new ones from hardware stores; the dealer should also have replacement parts for the few mechanical components that occasionally do fail. Other repairs (chart, right) call for adjusting parts rather than replacing them.

The most common problems of a window shade—excessive or inadequate tension in the spring that rolls the shade up—are easily solved. To reduce the tension, raise the shade all the way and pull the flat end pin out of its bracket; then unroll the shade about halfway by hand and replace the pin in the bracket. To increase the tension, pull the shade halfway down, take the flat pin from its bracket and roll the shade up by hand. Repeat these procedures until the tension is satisfactory.

## Diagnosing Venetian-Blind Troubles

| Symptoms | Causes | Remedies |
|---|---|---|
| Bottom slats not horizontal | Lift cord misaligned | Raise or lower one side of lift cord until slats are level; set new alignment with equalizer catch. |
| Slats do not tilt | Tilt cord not aligned in pulley | Rethread cord |
| | Tapes disengaged from tilt rod | Clip tapes to tilt tubes (metal blinds); staple tapes to tilt rod (wooden blinds) |
| | Worm gear sticks | Lubricate gear with light oil |
| | Worm wheel teeth disengaged from worm gear | Turn wheel by hand until teeth catch in gear |
| | Worm wheel or tilt rod is out of guides | Reposition wheel or rod |
| Lift cord does not lock | Incorrect operation of blind | Pull and release cord diagonally on one side, then the other to find position of lock |
| | Cord out of lift-cord lock | Rethread cord |
| Lift-cord lock catches too often or blind cannot be lowered | Incorrect operation of blind | Pull cord straight down and guide it straight up |

**The works of a Venetian blind.** Two cords regulate the tilt and height of the slats in a Venetian blind. The tilt cord, at the left side, is linked (inset)—by a pulley, a worm gear and a tilt rod—to the tapes at the front and back of the slats. Pulling the cord raises and lowers the tapes to change the tilt of the slats. In the metal blind shown here, the tapes are clipped to two short cylinders called tilt tubes, mounted on a metal tilt rod; in wooden blinds, the tapes are stapled to a wooden tilt rod.

The lift cord at the right side passes over pulleys in the headbox and is knotted under the bottom slat or bar. Pulling the cord straight down raises the bottom slat, stacking the others above it. An equalizer catch holds the ends of the cord in alignment to keep the bottom slat horizontal. The level of the bottom slat is fixed by a toothed lift-cord lock; when the cord is pulled diagonally, the teeth clamp it in place.

To dismantle a Venetian blind, remove the clamps or staples that fasten the tapes to the bottom slat or bar. Untie the knots at the ends of the lift cord and pull this cord free from the slats and pulleys. Pull the slats horizontally out of the tapes and detach the tapes from the tilt rod. For reassembly, reverse the procedure.

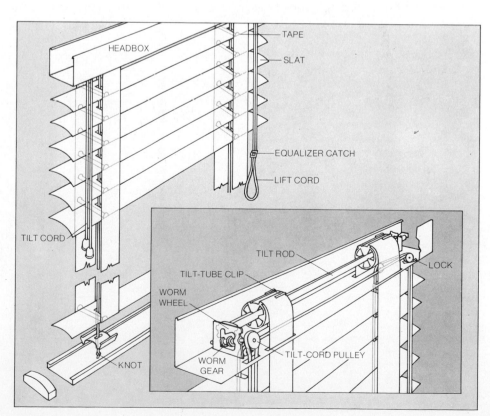

# Common Shutter Repairs

Because they are constantly adjusted to regulate light and provide privacy, interior wooden shutters are chronic candidates for surgery—but the surgery is generally minor. For example, the job of refastening a loose louver to the rod that sets the tilt of the louvers can be done without removing the shutter from its hinges. If the U-shaped pin that holds the louver to the rod has worked loose and fallen off, a thicker replacement pin, available from hardware stores, can be driven into the old pinholes.

Repairing a sagging shutter is almost as simple. Take the shutter from its hinges, unscrew the hinge plate, and plug the screw holes with wood filler or a matchstick, then screw the hinge plate back into place. The only special tool you may need for repairs is a set of bar clamps—clamps that adjust for length by sliding along a steel bar or piece of pipe—if you must reglue loose joints.

Shutters can, of course, be improved as well as repaired. To give shutters additional support and prevent them from sagging, professionals fasten thin rubber bumpers to the bottom of each panel, so that the window stool as well as the hinges supports the closed shutters. Use white bumpers to avoid smudging the stool.

Exterior wooden shutters are simpler in every way: they rarely have movable louvers and generally are nailed to the exterior walls to serve a purely decorative function. If a hinged exterior shutter sags, fill the screw holes of the hinges as you would on an interior shutter; if it does not close securely, install a hook-and-catch lock on the shutter and stool.

**Anatomy of an interior shutter.** Each panel of this two-tiered set of shutters consists of a glued frame and a set of movable louvers; other types have fixed louvers. In each tier, the panels are hinged to each other; the panel at the edge of the window is also hinged to a hanging strip that is attached to the window jamb. Pegs fitted into holes in the shutter frame support movable louvers; compression springs in two peg holes (inset) hold the louvers at the angle set by a tilt rod, which is attached to all the louvers by a set of U-shaped pins.

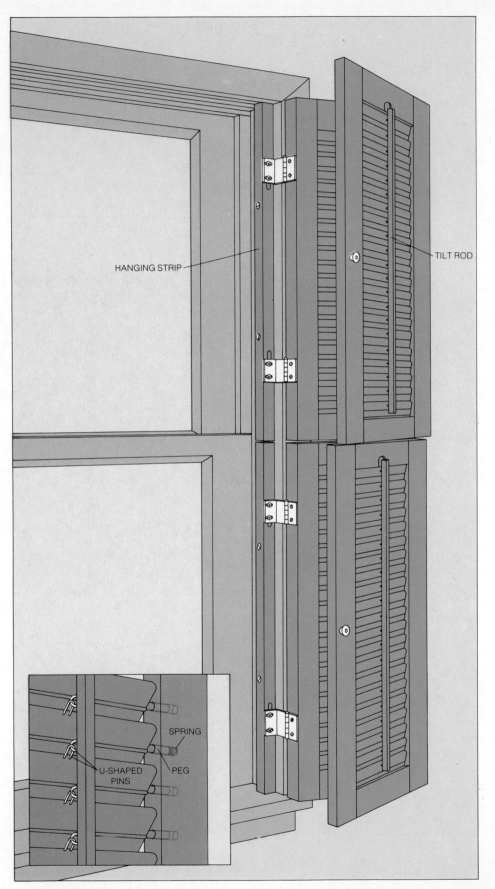

HANGING STRIP

TILT ROD

SPRING

PEG

U-SHAPED PINS

# Fixing Pins, Pegs and Joints

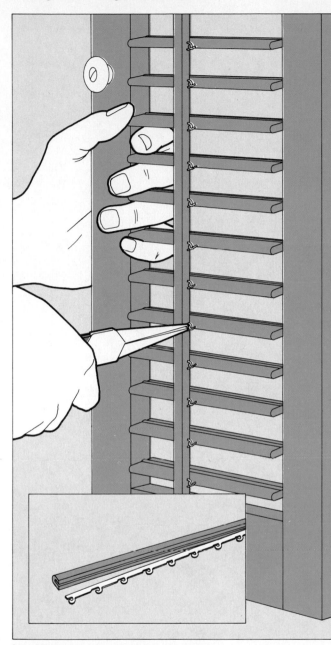

**Replacing a broken louver peg.** Unhook the louver from the tilt rod, pull it out of the shutter frame, and drill a ⅛-inch hole in the peg stub for the narrow end of a special replacement peg. Insert a spring and the new peg, wide end first, into the frame hole, holding the peg flush to the edge of the frame with a utility knife. Then slip the other peg into place on the opposite side of the frame, align the louver with the hole containing the spring and peg, and slide the knife out; the spring will push the replacement peg partway into the new hole in the louver.

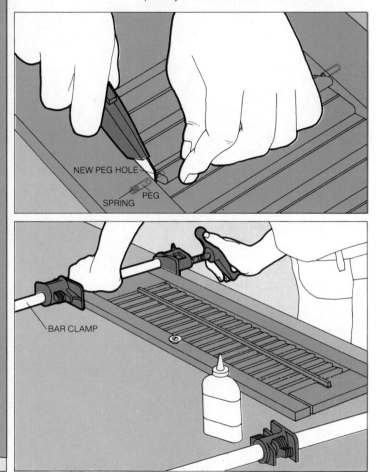

NEW PEG HOLE

SPRING    PEG

BAR CLAMP

**Attaching louvers to a tilt rod.** Set the louvers individually to a horizontal position and hold the flat side of the tilt rod against them. If the rod is wood, hold the louvers in place with the fingers of one hand, then use long-nose pliers to push new U-shaped pins through the rod pins and secure them in the louver pinholes. Replace rod pins in the same way.

Your tilt rod may consist of a one-piece, looped aluminum strip set in a wooden shaft *(inset)*. If a loop snaps off or is badly bent, bend all the loops open with long-nose pliers and remove the tilt rod. Pull the strip out of its channel in the rod, slide a new strip into place and, one by one, bend the strip loops over the louver pins.

**Gluing loose joints.** With the panel off its hinges, clamp the end opposite the loose joint and check the fit of the louver pegs in the sides of the frame; the best tool for clamping is the bar clamp illustrated. Replace missing compression springs, then push the frame together, leaving just enough space for the tip of a glue dispenser, and coat both sides of the loose joint with glue. Clamp the frame tightly, using a second clamp at the glued end, and wipe off excess glue immediately. Leave the clamps in place until the glue dries—usually overnight.

# Installing a Set of Shutters

Before you can hang a set of shutters, you must make a critical preliminary decision: whether to fasten the hanging strips, which support the shutters on adjustable hinges, to the window casings or to the jambs. A casing installation is the easier of the two—the strips are simply screwed to the face of the casings. Jamb installation, the method shown here, is a more painstaking job, but it is preferred by professionals because it produces a neater appearance, making the shutters fit inside the window opening rather than protrude into the room. The only special requirement is a jamb surface at least 1¼ inches wide to accommodate a hanging strip.

Although you can have shutters custom made to fit your windows, most installations are made with less expensive stock shutters, bought oversize and trimmed to a perfect fit before they are hung. These shutters come in widths from 6 to 15 inches in 1-inch increments, and in heights from 16 to 40 inches in 4-inch increments.

Because few windows are perfect rectangles, measure the length and width of each at three equidistant points, checking width between side jambs and height between the stool and the head jamb. Use the smallest measurement of length and width in the following calculations:

Subtract $7/16$ inch from the total width of each four-panel horizontal tier to allow for panel hinges and hanging strips. Subtract $3/8$ inch from the height for clearance between the shutters and the window frame; if you install two horizontal tiers of shutters, subtract another $3/16$ inch from their total height for clearance between tiers. Divide the final height figure by the number of top and bottom edges (two in a single-tier installation, four in a double-tier); divide the final width figure by the number of vertical panel edges. The resulting figures indicate the amount to trim from the height and width of each panel for a perfect fit. Generally, you can trim up to ½ inch from the side of a panel and as much as 2 inches from the top or bottom without weakening joints.

**1** **Marking the panels for trimming.** Align a complete set of shutter panels, interior side down, across two 1-by-2s on a workbench, butting the ends against a 2-by-4 nailed to the bench; then mark the panels with a pencil for the amount of trim, set a straightedge on the pencil marks and score the shutters along the straightedge with a utility knife. Score the opposite ends of the panels in the same way, but score the side edges individually.

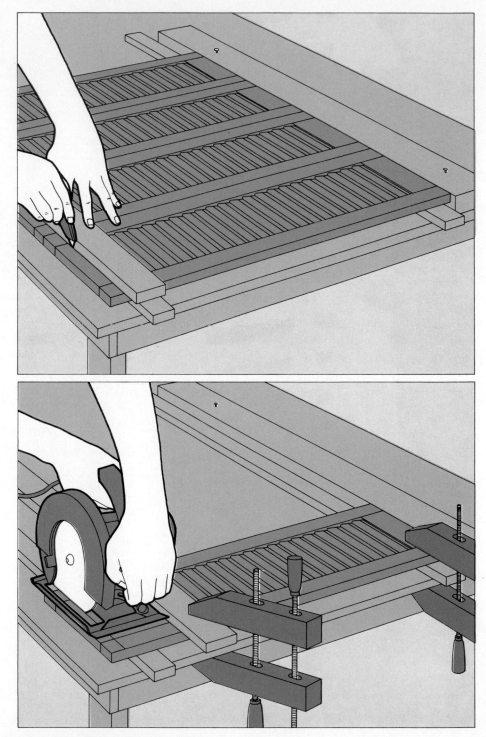

**2** **Trimming panels.** Clamp each panel over 1-by-2s, anchor a 1-by-4 guide strip to the panel with another clamp and saw along the strip. Sand the edges, then trim the hanging strips to match the height of the panels.

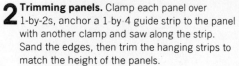

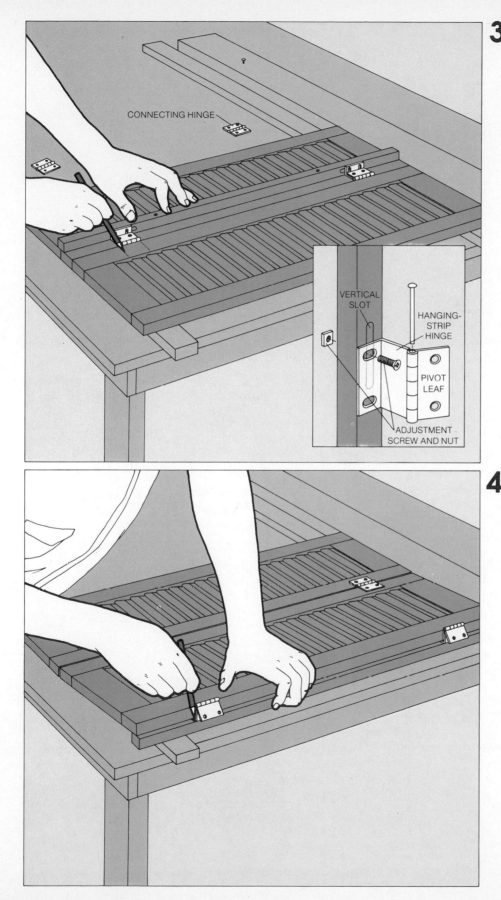

CONNECTING HINGE

VERTICAL
SLOT

HANGING-
STRIP
HINGE

PIVOT
LEAF

ADJUSTMENT
SCREW AND NUT

**3** **Hinging the panels.** Install the hinges on a hanging strip, placing each hinge-adjustment screw in the center of the vertical slot *(inset)*, then tightening the nut that secures it. Hold the strip against the back of the panels to be hinged and mark the locations of the hanging-strip hinges on the adjoining edges of the panels. Tape a penny between the panels near each hinge position to allow for clearance, align connecting hinges, pin sides up, with the marks you have made and mark the screw holes. Screw the connecting hinges into place.

**4** **Fitting the hanging-strip hinges.** Place the hanging strip in alignment under the end panel and mark the locations of the hanging-strip hinges on the panel edge. Detach the pivot leaves from the hinges by pulling out the pins, then set each leaf at the pencil marks, placing it flush with the back edge of the panel so that the pin side is toward the interior edge of the panel. Mark the locations of the screw holes, screw the pivot leaves to the panels and reassemble the hinges.

With a helper, hold each half of the shutter set against the window opening and check all clearances. Detach the shutters from the hanging strips and, if necessary, make additional trims.

VERTICAL
ADJUSTMENT
CHANNEL

HORIZONTAL
ADJUSTMENT
CHANNEL

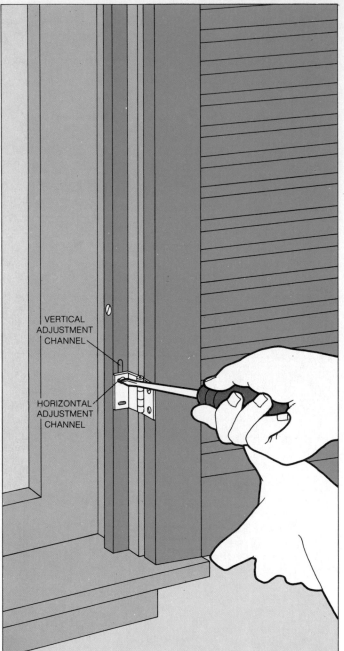

PENNY

STOOL

**5** **Installing the hanging strips.** With a penny spacer between the bottom of the hanging strip and the stool, place each strip flush with or slightly inside the edge of the jamb, then drill through the pilot holes in the strip into the jamb. Fasten the hanging strips to the jamb with the screws provided by the manufacturer and reattach the shutters.

**6** **Adjusting the shutters.** Starting with the lower tier of shutters, close the two sections and note the gap between them and between the shutters and the stool. Open the shutters, loosen the adjustment screw and nut in each hinge on the hanging strip, move the hinges vertically or horizontally to align the shutters, and tighten the screws. Adjust the shutter sections until there is an even gap the thickness of a penny between them and between the shutters and the stool. Adjust the upper tier in the same way.

Run a wood screw through the empty slot in each hanging-strip hinge into the hanging strip. Finally, install the hook-and-knob latch according to the manufacturer's instructions.

# Tricks for Replacing a Glass Block

For many years, after a boom that lasted from the 1930s into the 1950s, glass blocks were out of architectural fashion. Not until the mid-1970s did they begin to regain popularity. Their return to fashion may have been stimulated by a growing concern over energy costs (a hollow glass block is a far better insulator than sheet glass), but other virtues of the material also played a part. Glass blocks are a useful, often elegant cross between masonry and glass, offering some of the strength of masonry while transmitting almost as much light—usually diffused for privacy—as a pane of glass.

Though glass blocks are strong enough to guard against vandalism and burglary, they cannot support the weight of a structure above them; they must always be topped with a header or lintel. With this precaution, small numbers of glass blocks, covering an area of up to 25 square feet, can be installed in much the same way as ordinary cinder or concrete blocks, with a standard mortar mix: 1 part portland cement, 1 part lime and 4 parts sand. Larger areas need installation techniques generally left to professionals; and they require special hardware that ties the blocks to the surrounding structure, compensates for the different expansion rates of glass and other materials, and braces the blocks against wind.

Replacing a broken block requires no special hardware or skills, but the professional tricks at right make for a faster, neater job. Finding a replacement block is surprisingly easy: the standard sizes and designs have changed little since blocks were first popular, and a dealer (usually listed in the Yellow Pages under Glass Block, Structural) should be able to match the block you have.

**1** **Knocking out the broken block.** Tape heavy cloth over both sides of the damaged block and, wearing goggles and gloves, hammer the rest of the block inward, working from the center toward the edges. Remove the cloth and sweep out the broken glass. Use a stiff-bladed putty knife to pry off any pieces of glass stuck to the mortar, then carefully remove the mortar with a hammer and cold chisel; take care not to damage the surrounding blocks.

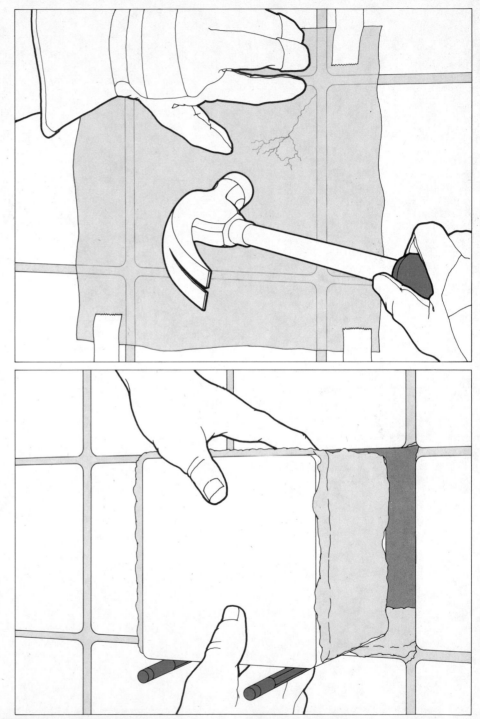

**2** **Mortaring in the new block.** Spread a ¼-inch layer of mortar on the top and sides of the new block and on the bottom of the cavity. Lay two dowels or ordinary pencils in the mortar bed to support the new block and then slide the block into position on top of the dowels. Pack additional mortar into the joints if necessary and allow the mortar to set for about an hour. Remove the dowels, fill in the holes they leave in the mortar and shape concave joints with a thin rod or a jointing tool. Clean off any excess mortar with a wet cloth.

# The Glazier's Craft: Cutting and Setting Glass

Someday, by the law of averages, a budding Babe Ruth will drive a baseball through your living-room window. If you learn a few tricks of reglazing, you will be able to replace the shattered pane almost as easily as he broke it. Using the same basic glazing techniques, you may be able to refit your windows with insulated, or double-glazed, glass—two panes sealed at the edges, with inert gas between them. The panes, which require a sash channel at least 1 inch wide, come in a range of precut sizes; panes smaller than 12 by 12 inches generally must be custom-made. Single-glazed panes will be cut to size by most glass and hardware stores, but it may be more convenient and economical to cut your own.

Special tools for working with glass include a glass cutter (a carbide scoring wheel holds an edge better than a wheel of tungsten steel) and a pair of wide-nose glass pliers *(page 53, Step 2)*. To install a pane in a wooden sash, you will need wedge-shaped fasteners called glazier's points to hold the pane in place, linseed oil to soften old putty and coat the inside of the frame (uncoated wood draws oil from new glazing compound and makes it brittle), and glazing compound to cushion the glass in the frame and make a watertight seal.

Use a latex-base compound to glaze insulated glass—though oil-base compounds are less expensive, they rot the sealant that holds the double panes together. For a metal sash, you generally need spring clips *(page 55, top)* rather than glazier's points; some models require gaskets or moldings.

Before you cut a windowpane, practice on scrap glass to get a feel for the amount of pressure needed to score the glass for a clean cut. Too much pressure will crack the glass; too little will only scratch it. A rasping sound as you draw the cutter across the glass indicates that the pressure is right.

To determine the size of a replacement pane, measure the inside of the frame after you have removed the remains of the old pane and all old putty, then subtract ⅛ inch from each dimension to allow for expansion. Have a professional make any cut longer than 4 feet: beyond that length, glass is difficult to handle, and a slip of the cutter will be costly.

## Safety Tips for Working with Glass

Cutting and handling glass are not dangerous if you take the following precautions:

☐ Wear heavy leather work gloves when handling loose panes or fragments of glass.

☐ Wear safety goggles when removing broken glass or cutting glass.

☐ Work with a helper whenever you carry panes larger than 4 by 4 feet.

☐ Transport glass in several layers of newspaper on a padded surface (an old rug will do). Secure the pane by wedging a pillow at each side.

☐ Have a professional deliver any pane you cannot lay flat in your car.

☐ Before storing panes, mark them with a grease pencil or masking tape so they are easily seen.

☐ Cut glass on a padded surface.

☐ Immediately after cutting glass, brush fragments off the work surface.

☐ If the window is in a hard-to-reach location, remove the sash *(page 12)* and work on a flat surface.

## Clearing the Frame

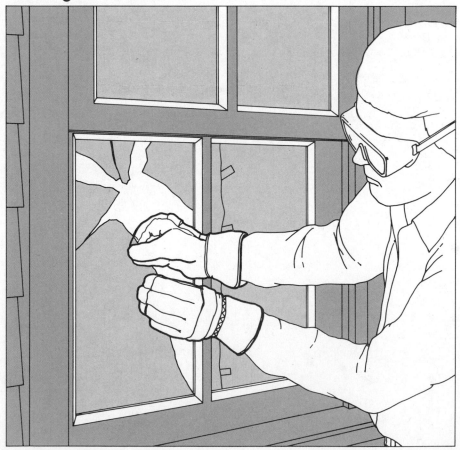

**1** **Removing broken glass.** Tape newspaper to the inside of the frame to catch glass fragments; then, from outside the house, work the shards of glass back and forth to free them.

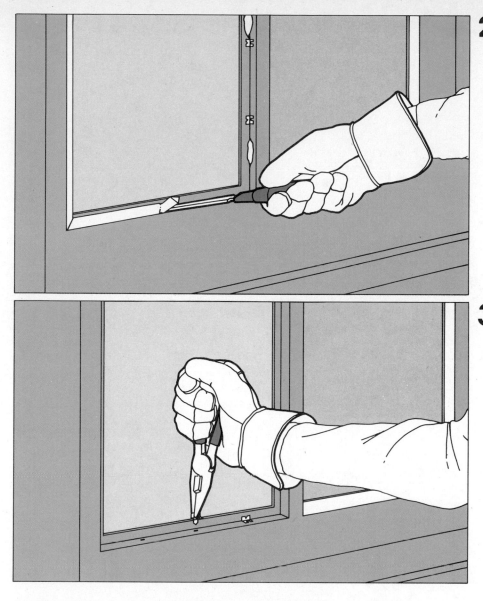

**2 Removing glazing compound.** Brush the old glazing compound with linseed oil, let the oil soak in for a half hour, then scrape off the softened compound with a wood chisel.

If oil does not soften the compound sufficiently, run the tip of a heated soldering iron lightly back and forth along the compound, then scrape the sash clean with the chisel. Caution: do not touch the tip of the iron to the sash.

**3 Smoothing the channel.** Pull the glazier's points out of the frame with long-nose pliers and remove loose fragments of glass and glazing compound with a wire brush. Sand the channel smooth and brush it with linseed oil.

## Cutting a Rectangular Pane

**1 Scoring the glass.** Lay the glass on a padded surface, such as a scrap of carpet or a sheet of thin foam rubber. Brush linseed oil on the area to be scored and set a straightedge along the cut line. Slanting the cutter toward you and holding it between your first and second fingers, pull it along the straightedge, starting about $1/16$ inch from the edge of the glass, to score the glass in one smooth motion. Caution: do not go back over the score line—a double score will cause the glass to break with an uneven edge.

**2** **Deepening the score line.** While a helper tilts one edge of the pane up from the work surface, tap the glass lightly along the underside of the score line with the ball at the end of the glass cutter; the blows will deepen the score. Then proceed to Step 3 immediately.

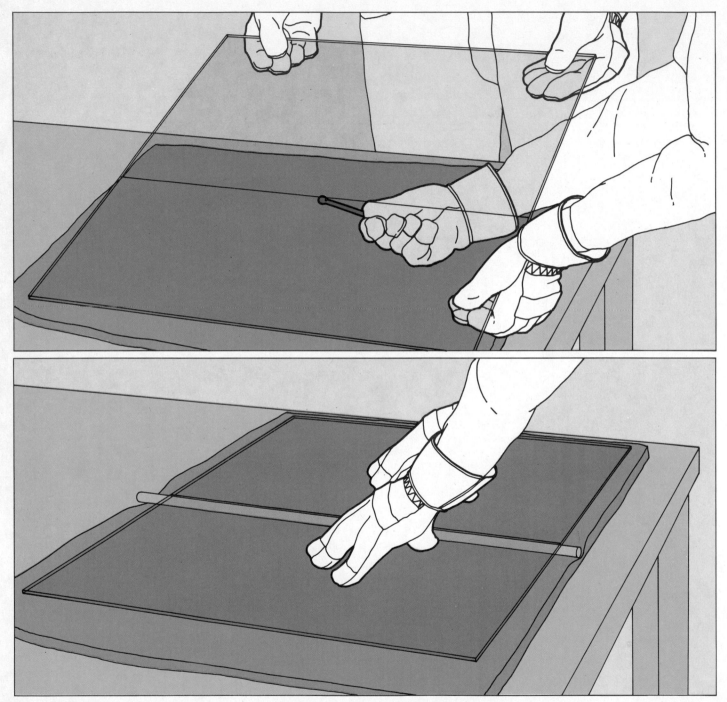

**3** **Snapping the glass.** Place a thin rod, such as a dowel—at least as long as the score line—on the work surface. Position the score line directly over the rod and press down firmly on both sides of the score; the glass should snap cleanly. Use 240-grit silicon-carbide sandpaper or an emery stone to smooth the new edge.

## A Template for a Curved Cut

**1 Making the score.** Cut a hardboard template to the desired shape of the pane and set it on the glass; for the most common type of curved pane, which has one straight edge, align the template's straight side with the edge of the glass. While a helper holds the template firmly with both hands, make the score in a single motion from one end of the curve to the other.

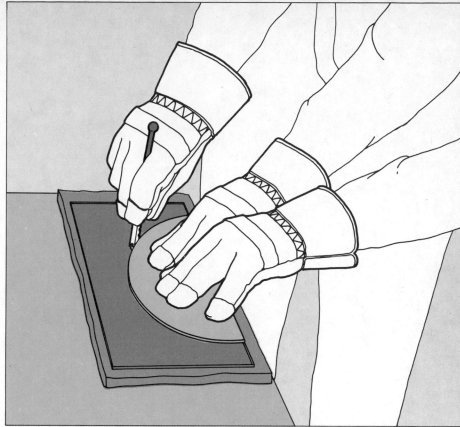

**2 Snapping the curve.** Scribe several radiating scores from the curve to the edge of the glass and tap under all the score lines (*opposite, Step 2*); then hold one edge of the glass over the end of the worktable and snap off the scored segments with a pair of glass pliers. Smooth the edge with sandpaper or emery stone.

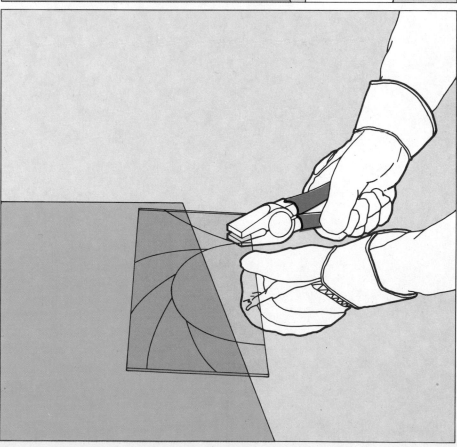

## Setting Glass
## in a Wooden Sash

**1 Lining the frame.** Roll glazing compound between your palms into strips about ¼ inch thick and press the strips into the channels in which the pane of glass will rest. Add more compound until you have filled the channels completely.

**2 Securing the glass.** Press the pane of glass firmly into the glazing compound and scrape off excess compound with a utility knife or a razor blade; then fasten the pane securely in place with glazier's points pushed into the frame with a putty knife. Use two points on each edge for a frame up to 10 inches square, one point every 4 inches for a larger frame.

**3 Beveling the glazing compound.** Press additional strips of glazing compound around the frame, then smooth the strips with a putty knife into a neat bevel that runs from the face of a sash or a muntin (sash divider) onto the glass. As you work, dip the knife in water from time to time to prevent it from sticking to the compound. When the compound has hardened—in five to seven days—paint it to match the frame, extending the coat of paint $1/16$ inch onto the glass for a weathertight seal.

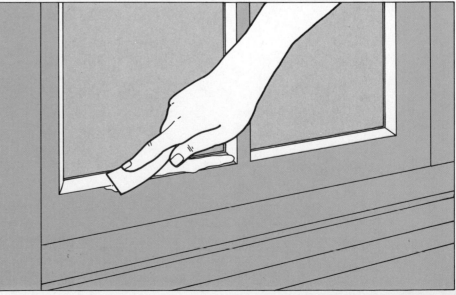

# Three Ways of Glazing a Metal Sash

**A set of spring clips.** Some windows have flexible V-shaped metal clips to secure the glass, instead of glazier's points. With such a window, work on the inside of the frame; take out the old glass and glazing compound (*pages 50-51*) and remove the spring clips that secure the glass by pinching them and pulling them out of the holes in the frame. Paint the empty channel. When the paint has dried, lay a thin bead of glazing compound in the channel, then press the new pane firmly into the compound and replace the spring clips. Seal the pane with a bevel of glazing compound (*opposite, Step 3*).

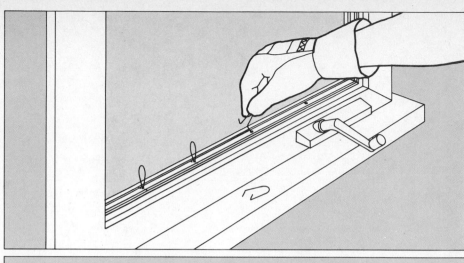

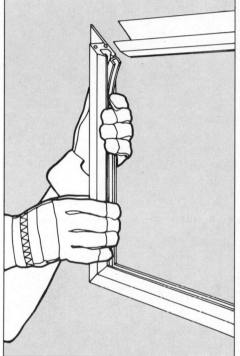

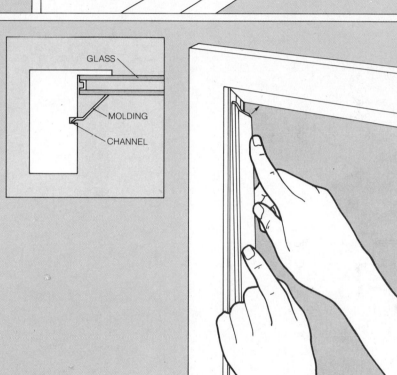

**Rubber gaskets.** In some metal windows, the glass rests in four rubber gaskets, U-shaped in cross section, and the sash comes apart for removal of the gaskets and glass. The model shown has screws at the top and bottom of one vertical edge of the sash. From outside the house, unfasten the screws and pull the side piece from the rest of the frame, remove the old glass from the gaskets, brushing out fragments with a wire brush, and pull the gaskets out of their channels. Fit the gaskets on the new pane, slide the pane into the frame and refasten the side piece. In another popular model, the gaskets are sandwiched between the halves of a split sash, and the retaining screws are at the corners of the sash face. In this type, replacement of the glass is done from inside. Remove the screws and pull the inner half of the sash away to get at the gaskets and glass.

**Snap-out plastic moldings.** Insulated glass is secured in a common type of metal window by four beveled moldings (*inset*) that snap into channels in the frame. When the glass must be replaced, put on gloves, remove any broken glass, then loosen the end of one piece of molding by inserting the tip of a putty knife where two strips meet; pull the strip from the channel with your hands. Remove the other strips in the same way. Brush loose glass from the frame and set the new pane in place. Then push the beveled sides of the two short moldings into their channels, one at a time, pressing them into place with your fingers; fit the long strips last. If the moldings show even slight damage, install replacements, available at glass dealers.

**Supports for two openings.** An L-shaped steel beam called a lintel sustains the load above the door or window opening in a brick-veneer or solid-masonry wall; its wooden counterpart, a sandwich of beams and plywood called a header, does the same job in wood-frame walls. Below each beam is the tool that fastens it in place—a trowel for masonry, a hammer for wood.

A new door or window begins with a hole in a wall—and for some homeowners, that fact alone justifies calling in a professional. Cutting or smashing a large hole in the thin protective skin of a house seems an awesome undertaking, until you know exactly how to do it. In a house with wood, aluminum or stucco siding, making an opening is a simple matter of removing the vertical supports, called studs, inside the house, and then going outdoors to cut through the siding with a saw. In a solid-masonry wall, you must break out rows of bricks or concrete blocks with a chisel and a light sledge hammer. And in a frame house with a brick veneer, you make the opening using a combination of both methods.

Such a hole does not threaten the structure of the house. Extensive bracing is not needed unless the wall you breach is a bearing wall, which supports part of the weight of the house, or unless you are making an opening more than 40 inches wide in a solid-masonry or brick-veneer wall. Such walls require temporary supports until a strong lateral beam—wooden in a wood-frame house, steel in brick veneer or solid masonry—can be installed as a permanent brace. In a frame house, the wooden beam, called a header, forms part of a rough frame for the door or window; in a solid-masonry house, steel headers called lintels must be put in; and in a brick-veneer house both a wooden header and a steel lintel are required.

In most communities you need a permit for this kind of work. The local building department will review plans for the opening (they can be rough sketches drawn to scale) to make sure the rough frame is strong enough to support the load above the opening. At least one official inspection of the job is required, and in some localities inspections are made at several stages.

Stockpile everything you need, including the door or window you plan to put in and lumber for temporary supports and the rough frame; for an opening in masonry, order the lintel or lintels cut to length ahead of time. And for any type of opening, get a sheet of heavy-duty polyethylene plastic to shield the exposed opening from the wind or a sudden rain. For an exterior door with a threshold or sill more than a foot off the ground, plan a temporary guardrail inside the opening to block it until the door is in place and the gap below it has been filled. Store materials in the garage, if you can; otherwise, use the room in which you will make the opening—because the work is dirty, you will have to clear this room of furniture in any case. Recruit helpers in advance to measure the opening and heft heavy beams and lengths of lumber. And remember that after the job is done, you will find yourself with a small mountain of debris and may need to call for a special garbage pickup.

# Installing a Simple Frame in a Wooden Structure

To add a door or window to a house of wooden construction, you must first cut an opening in a wall and fit the opening with a wooden frame, called a rough frame. The following pages deal with a wide opening and rough frame for a door or window in an exterior bearing wall—a wall that supports the floor above it or the roof. This job requires temporary shoring and a heavy permanent framework around the opening, as well as precise cuts in the sheathing and siding. But the techniques apply to an opening in any wall. The only variations are simplifications—no special support or heavy framework is needed in a nonbearing

wall, and less precision in cutting is required in an interior wall.

To determine whether a wall is a bearing wall, study the floor plan of your house. Nonbearing partitions are generally short and parallel to joists and rafters. Bearing walls are longer and perpendicular to joists; they usually bear directly on one another and bear on girders or solid walls in the basement or crawl space.

All nonbearing walls are built in much the same way, with one-story vertical studs between horizontal bottom and top plates. But bearing walls can be either platform framed or balloon framed —terms that refer to alternate ways of

building a house. In platform framing *(below, left)*, the most common type, the stories of the house are assembled like a stack of separate boxes: the first-story joists and subfloor (the platform) are assembled first, then the first-story walls are put up; the second story rests on the first, and so on for succeeding stories. In balloon framing, the house is built like an open box with shelves inside. Long studs, running all the way from the sill of the foundation to the rafters, are assembled first; then the first- and second-floor joists are fitted between them.

Balloon framing *(pages 63-65)* requires additional shoring while you make the

## The Basic Houses: Platform and Balloon

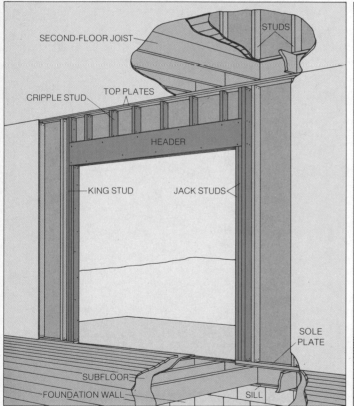

**Platform framing.** A header—a stiff sandwich made from two large boards and a plywood spacer—bridges the top of this door opening. At the sides, extra full-length studs called king studs are toenailed to the sole and top plates and nailed to the ends of the header. Cripple studs inserted beneath the top plate transmit the weight of the roof and second floor down to the header; short jack studs carry the load from the ends of the header to the sole plate.

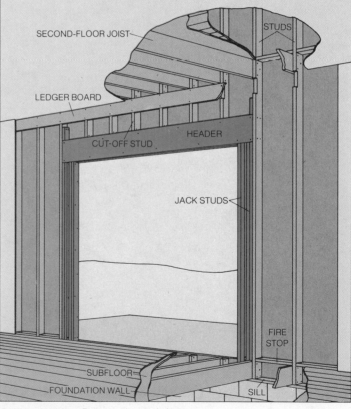

**Balloon framing.** Because the studs in a balloon-frame wall are so long, you cannot insert new king studs; the nearest existing stud beyond each side of the opening is used as a king stud. The extra-long header is supported by jack studs in the ordinary way. Additional jack studs are installed at the actual edges of the opening. All the jack studs run past the floor joists to the sill plate. The studs within the opening are cut to fit the top of the header.

opening and different framing. If you can see studs rising alongside the joists in the basement or crawl space, your house is the balloon type; if no studs can be seen, the house is the platform type.

You can simplify the framing job by adapting the opening to the special features of your own house. For example, you can save labor by locating the opening at an existing stud. Trace the routes of the cables, pipes and ducts inside the wall you are opening; you may be able to avoid them rather than going to the trouble of moving them. If the top of the rough frame—the header—for the opening would be within 2 inches of the top plate, you can eliminate intermediate "cripple" studs by making a wider header and setting it against the top plate.

The peculiarities of your house may create special difficulties. Depending on when your wall was built, it may have studs wider than the modern standard. If this is the case, remove the old studs carefully and reuse them or cut modern 2-by-6s down to fit. In a brick-veneer house, remove the layer of veneer (pages 66-69) before beginning work on the wood frame. And if you are cutting an opening in a second-story wall, rent scaffolding to get at the exterior, and erect temporary shoring (page 60) on the first floor as well as the second.

Other difficulties may arise from structural hazards created by an opening—but these problems are usually surmountable without unusual effort. If a particularly heavy load bears directly above an open-

ing, it is advisable to get an architect or structural engineer to determine the header size you need. You should also consult an expert if an opening in an exterior wall is within 4 feet of the corner of the house, or if you find steel columns, wooden posts or diagonal bracing inside a wall. Such cases may require extra support that an engineer can design and that you can install in the course of the job.

The job itself starts with the purchase of the new door or window. Locate the nearest studs beyond the sides of the opening and snap vertical chalk lines from floor to ceiling along the facing edges of these studs. Turn off electrical power in the vicinity, then cut through the wall along the chalk lines with a circular saw and remove the wall covering.

## The Basic Headers: Wood-Core and Steel-Core

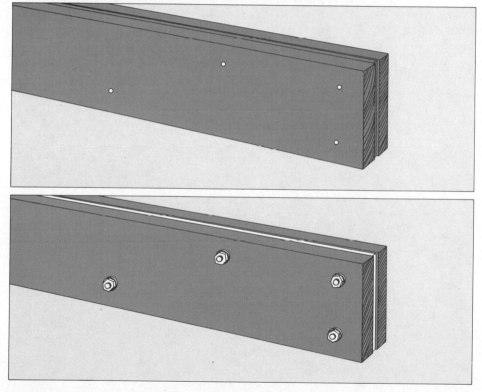

**A wood header.** The most common header, cheaper than a solid-wood beam and at least as strong, is a sandwich made of two structural-grade boards 2 inches thick and a piece of ½-inch plywood. For a bearing wall, determine the width of the board (chart, below) and cut a matching piece of ½-inch plywood. Cut all three pieces to length and fasten them together from both sides with staggered 16-penny nails every 10 inches. For a nonbearing wall, build the sandwich from 2-by-4s if the opening is less than 6 feet wide, 2-by-6s if it is wider.

**A steel-reinforced header.** For extremely long spans or where a wooden header of the required width will not fit between the top of the opening and the top plate of the wall, reduce the width of the header by bolting two boards to a steel plate. Check your local building code to determine the thickness of the plate, the width of the boards and the spacing of the boltholes. Have a steel supplier cut the plate to length and make the holes. Use the plate as a template to drill matching holes in both boards and bolt the sandwich together with machine bolts.

## Matching a Header to Load and Span

| Load above opening | Span in feet | | | | |
|---|---|---|---|---|---|
| | 4 | 6 | 8 | 10 | 12 |
| Roof only | 2x4 | 2x6 | 2x8 | 2x10 | 2x12 |
| One story | 2x6 | 2x8 | 2x10 | 2x12 | — |
| Two stories | 2x10 | 2x10 | 2x12 | — | — |

**Choosing the right header.** To find the dimensions of the boards for a header, match the span of the opening (shown along the top of the chart) with the load above the opening (shown in the left-hand column); for a span between those listed, use the column for the next larger span. If the space for your span and load is blank, use a steel-reinforced header (above) in a size specified by your local building code.

# Framing for a Door in a Platform Wall

**1 Supporting the load.** Erect and shim a temporary partition parallel to the planned opening and about 4 feet from the wall. To assemble this partition, first nail a double 2-by-4 sole plate, 4 feet longer than the width of the new door or window, to the floor; set a 2-by-4 top plate beside the sole plate and mark both plates for 2-by-4 studs at 16-inch intervals. Cut studs 6¼ inches shorter than the distance between floor and ceiling, nail them to the top plate and nail a second 2-by-4 to the plate. With a helper, set the assembly on the sole plate and plumb the end studs in both directions, and toenail the studs to the bottom plate.

Drive shim shingles between the double top plate and the ceiling at the ceiling joist locations, shimming until the partition fits tightly and immovably. Attach a 1-by-4 brace diagonally across the partition, from the floor at one end to the ceiling at the other end, nailing the brace to each stud. If your house has a basement or crawl space beneath the partition, support the floor joists with a horizontal 4-by-6 beam supported by 4-by-4 posts (*page 72, Step 5*).

DOUBLE TOP PLATE

SHIMS

DOUBLE SOLE PLATE

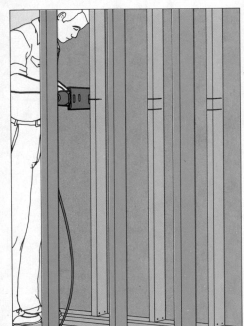

JACK-STUD LOCATIONS

KING-STUD LOCATION

**2 Removing the studs.** With a saber saw, make two cuts about an inch apart through the middle of each stud within the planned opening. Knock out the 1-inch pieces and complete the cuts with a wood chisel if necessary. Pry the studs away from the sheathing with a utility bar. Cut off the nails that protrude from the top and bottom plates with carpenter's nippers.

**3 Laying out the framework.** Measure between the outer edges of the side jambs of the finished door or window, add 1 inch (or the shimming space specified by the manufacturer) and draw lines this far apart on the sole plate, centered on the desired location of the finished unit. For an opening more than 6 feet wide, draw lines 1½ and 3 inches beyond each original line, to mark for double jack studs, and a fourth line another 1½ inches away, for the king stud (*inset*). For an opening less than 6 feet wide—which needs only single jack studs—draw lines 1½ and 3 inches beyond each original line. Drop a plumb bob from the top plate to the king-stud lines and draw matching lines across the top plate. Toenail 2-by-4 king studs between the plates.

**4** **Putting in the jack studs.** For a door, measure from the bottom of the threshold to the top of the side jamb, add ½ inch (or the dimension specified for shimming space by the manufacturer) and mark each king stud at this total height above the subfloor. For a window, measure from the finish floor to the bottom of the head jamb in an existing window in the room, add the distance between the bottom of the head jamb and the top of the side jamb of the new unit and mark each king stud the total distance up from the finish door. Cut 2-by-4 jack studs to the length between the mark on each king stud and the sole plate. For each side of an opening wider than 6 feet, use a pair of 2-by-4s nailed together with tenpenny nails every 12 inches; for a smaller opening, single jack studs do. Nail the jack studs to the plate and the stud.

**5** **Installing the header.** Make a header of the size required by the opening (*page 59*), and, with a helper, fit it snugly between the king studs and on the jack studs. Nail through the king studs into the ends of the header; toenail up through the jack studs into the bottom of the header.

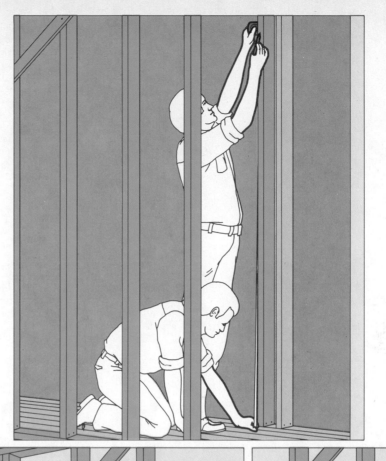

**6** **Putting in cripple studs.** If there is a gap between the header and the top plate of the wall, cut 2-by-4 cripple studs to fit. Nail a cripple stud to each king stud, set additional cripples in place of the studs you removed and toenail all the cripples to the top plate and the header.

## Completing the Rough Frame for a Window

**Adding a sill.** To install the rough sill and cripple studs that support the finished window sill, first measure the height of your window unit from the top of the side jamb to the point where the bottom of the finished sill will meet the siding. Add 2 inches if the window is less than 40 inches wide, 3½ inches if it is wider, and mark the jack studs at this total distance down from the header. Cut cripple studs to fit between the sole plate and the marks. Nail a cripple stud to each jack stud, then set a 2-by-4 rough sill on the cripples and toenail it to the jack studs. Place a cripple stud at each mark left by the old studs, nailing down through the sill into the top end and toenailing the bottom. If the opening is wider than 40 inches, nail a second horizontal 2-by-4 over the first.

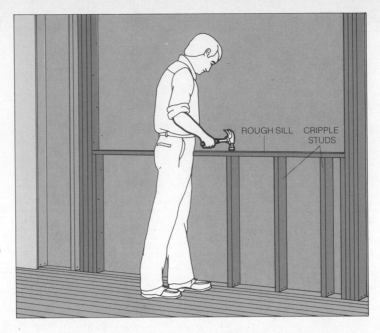

## Cutting through the Wall

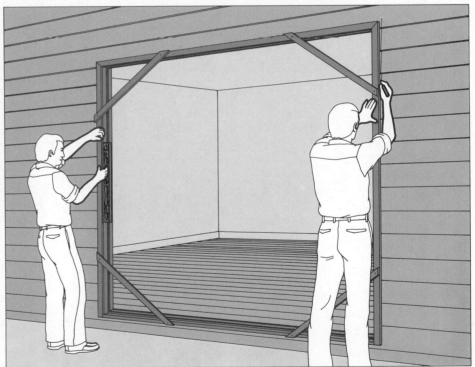

**1** **Cutting the opening.** For a door, drill pilot holes through the sheathing from inside at the corners of the rough frame. Outside, mark the siding 1½ inches below the bottom holes and draw lines connecting the marks and holes, using a straightedge. Cut through the sheathing and siding with a circular saw; wear goggles and a respirator. Cut through stucco with a masonry blade; otherwise use an old wood-cutting blade. Cut through the sole plate along the jack studs and remove the plate.

Make a window opening the same way, but drill the lower pilot holes ¾ inch above the rough sill and do not remove the sole plate.

**2** **Trimming the siding.** Cut back the siding around the opening so that the brickmold of the finished unit will rest against the sheathing of the wall with its edges ⅛ inch from the siding. For a large unit like the sliding door shown above, which requires precise fitting, enlist the aid of a helper to set the new unit in the opening, with its brickmold tight against the siding. Level the threshold or sill with shims, if necessary, and shim the side jambs until they are perfectly plumb. Trace the outline of the brickmold onto the siding. Set a circular saw to the thickness of the siding, cut along the outside of the lines—taking care not to cut through the sheathing—and pry away the cut siding.

For a small unit, it may be easier to mark the siding from measurements. Measure the width and height of the unit. Mark these dimensions on the siding at the sides, top and bottom of the opening, extend the marks with a level and a long straightedge and cut back the siding.

# Additional Support for a Balloon Wall

In balloon framing—standard until about 1930, and still used today in some frame houses that are veneered with stucco or brick—the exterior walls and interior bearing walls have long studs (visible from the basement or crawl space) that run from the sill plate of the foundation to the top plate of the second floor. The first-floor joists rest on the sill, while the second-story joists rest on a horizontal ledger board set into notches in the studs; both sets of joists are also nailed to the sides of the studs.

Making an opening in a balloon-type wall differs from making one in the platform type (preceding pages) in two respects. In addition to a temporary shoring partition (page 60, Step 1) to support the second-floor joists, you must also temporarily shore the studs themselves and the roof by bolting a horizontal board, called a whaler, to each stud.

Another difference arises from the sheer length of balloon-frame studs. Because you cannot slip new king studs into the wall at the sides of the opening, you must use two existing studs, one on each side of the opening, as king studs, then bridge the gap between the two with an extra-long header. Extra sets of jack studs are inserted at the actual sides of the opening to complete the framing.

## Whalers and Wide Headers to Carry the Load

**1 Supporting the studs.** Have a helper hold a whaler—a 2-by-8 about 2 feet longer than the width of the planned opening—against the studs and the ceiling, and nail it to the studs at each end. Then, about 2 inches above the bottom of the whaler, fasten it to each stud with a ⅜-inch lag bolt. Nail a short 2-by-8 plank flat on the floor beneath each end of the whaler and cut a 4-by-4 post to fit between the whaler and each plank. Plumb the posts, shim them tight against the whaler and toenail them in place. Support the joists above the opening (page 60, Step 1) and the joists beneath the floor (page 72, Step 5).

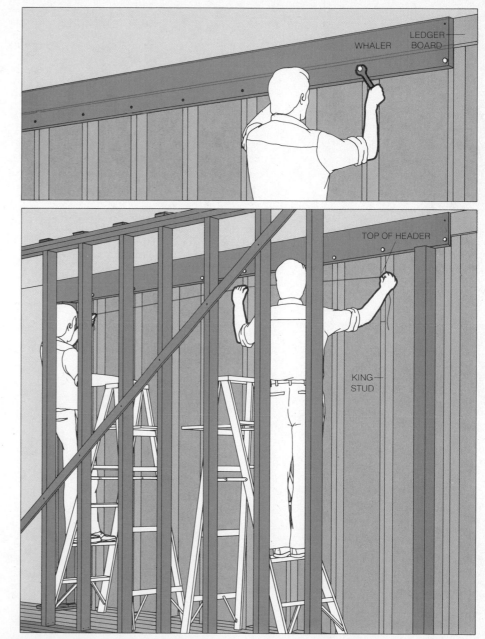

**2 Cutting the studs.** Mark the heights of the header top and header bottom on the existing studs that will serve as the king studs (page 61, Step 4) and, with a helper, snap a chalk line between the marks for the header top. Using a pencil and combination square, extend the line across the sides of the intervening studs and cut each stud along the line with a saber saw. Pry out the fire stop between the king stud and the nearest stud or floor joist. For a door, cut each stud within the opening about 6 inches above the floor; for a window, cut each stud about 3 feet below the cuts for the top of the header. Pry out the cut pieces.

**JACK STUDS** | **KING STUD**

**JOIST**

**3** **Nailing the jack studs.** Measure down from the header-bottom marks on the two existing studs that you are using as king studs to the joist or sill plate below it, cut 2-by-4 jack studs to these lengths and nail the jack studs to the king studs. For an opening more than 6 feet wide, nail a second jack stud to each of the first ones; if the first stud bears on a joist, run the second down past it to the sill plate (*inset*). Make and install the header (*page 61, Step 5*) and toenail the cut-off studs above the header to the top of the header. Nail a 2-by-4 about 1 foot long vertically to the side of each king stud, directly above the header.

**4** **Adding jack studs.** Mark the bottom and side of the header for the width of the rough opening and the positions of the extra jack studs at the sides of the actual opening (*page 60, Step 3*), then drop a plumb line from the header at each mark and have a helper draw corresponding lines on the floor. Knock out the fire stops in the marked stud space. If the extra jack studs are obstructed by the old stud, cut the stud and pry out the pieces. Make doubled jack studs the same length as those of Step 3, toenail them at the marks and nail a fire stop between the two sets of jack studs. Remove the whaler and the temporary shoring partition.

# Trimming the Studs

**Adding the sill for a door.** Drill pilot holes at the corners of the opening, with the bottom holes at the level of the subfloor, and cut the opening and trim the siding (*page 62, Steps 1 and 2*); then knock out the fire stops within the opening and cut the ends of the studs within the opening flush with the top of the joists. Extend the subfloor to the outside of the wall with a sill—a board as thick as the subfloor (usually ¾ inch), as wide as the studs and as long as the width of the rough opening. Nail this extension to the joists and to the jack studs at each end.

**Adding a window sill.** Cut off the existing studs at the bottom of the opening so that you can use them as cripple studs. Start by marking the jack studs at the height for the bottom of the rough sill (*page 62*), use the marks as guides to snap a chalk line on the intervening studs, then cut the studs at the lines with a saber saw. Nail an extra cripple stud to each jack stud between the sill plate and the mark for the rough sill, and nail the rough sill to the cripple studs.

After cutting the opening and trimming the siding (*page 62, Steps 1 and 2*), replace the fire stops you removed.

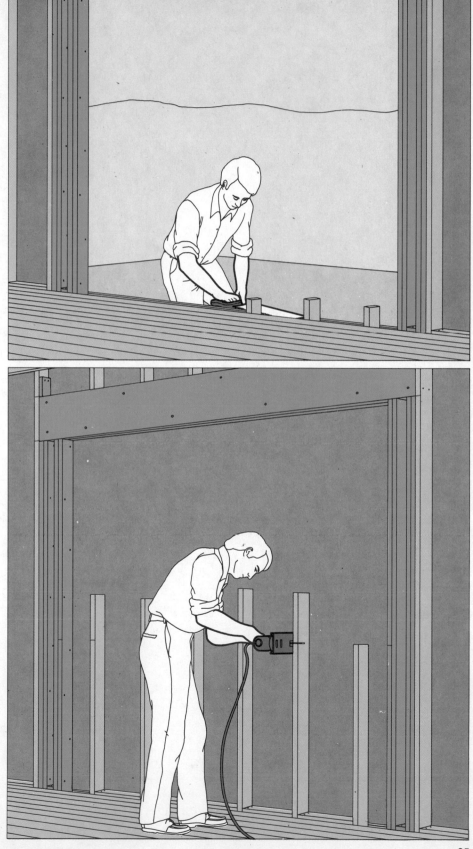

# How to Break an Opening through a Masonry Wall

Fashioning a wide door or window opening in brick veneer or solid masonry differs from providing an opening in wood siding. Part of the difference arises from the advisability of making the opening along mortar lines, since mortar is easier to cut than brick or block. This requires adjustments in the opening size.

Ideally, a rough opening would be ⅜ inch wider than the width of the new window or door unit, measured to the outside of the exterior casings, called brickmolds; and ¼ inch taller than the height, measured from the bottom of the threshold or sill to the top of the head brickmold. But if the mortar joints do not fall at the ideal positions, make the opening larger, using the next available joint. The gap between masonry and the top of the brickmold will be filled with caulking and wooden trim strips. Any gap at the sides is filled with brick.

To start the opening, score only the horizontal mortar joints at the sides of the marked opening. When all of the whole bricks within the opening are removed, a series of notches—what professional masons call a saw-tooth pattern—will remain. To fill the gaps in the saw-tooth pattern, you will have to cut some of the old bricks into odd-sized sections called bats. To make a bat, score a brick with a cold chisel. Then place the brick on a bed of sand and hammer the chisel sharply along the line; the brick will break cleanly. Before rebricking around the opening, take a sample of the existing mortar to a masonry supplier. He should be able to recommend a mix that will more or less match the color and texture of the old mortar.

Another difference in working with masonry is introduced by its weight—a brick weighs about 4 pounds; an 8-inch concrete block, 30 pounds. Instead of wooden headers, you must use one or more L-shaped steel beams, called lintels, over the opening to support the masonry above—one for an opening in brick veneer, two or three for solid masonry—and the dimensions of each lintel depend upon the span it must cover. Use the chart below to determine the size and number of lintels you need, and have them cut to order, 16 inches wider than the opening, by a steel-supply house. For an opening through solid masonry, you also must reinforce the brick or blocks with temporary crossbeams until the lintels are in position (pages 70-71).

Consult local building codes and obtain a construction permit before you begin the job. On the job, wear safety goggles whenever you must score, split or cut bricks and wear a respirator when you work on masonry with power tools.

## Choosing a Lintel

| Opening width (feet) | Lintel size (inches) Exterior | Interior |
|---|---|---|
| up to 4 | 3½ × 3½ × ⁵⁄₁₆ | 3½ × 3½ × ⁵⁄₁₆ |
| 5 | 3½ × 3½ × ⁵⁄₁₆ | 5 × 3½ × ⁵⁄₁₆ |
| 6 | 4 × 3½ × ⁵⁄₁₆ | 5 × 3½ × ⅜ |
| 7 | 4 × 3½ × ⁵⁄₁₆ | 6 × 4 × ⅜ |
| 8 | 5 × 3½ × ⁵⁄₁₆ | 7 × 4 × ⅜ |
| 9 | 5 × 3½ × ⅜ | 8 × 4 × ⁷⁄₁₆ |
| 10 | 6 × 3½ × ⅜ | 8 × 4 × ½ |

**Choosing the right lintel.** Use this table to order L-shaped steel lintels 16 inches longer than the width of the opening. In the second and third columns the first figure indicates the height of a lintel's vertical flange; the second, the depth of its horizontal flange; and the third, the thickness of the steel.

Most brick houses have only a veneer of masonry over a frame structure; they need only exterior lintels. Solid-masonry walls require lintels inside and out. For an 8-inch wall of solid masonry, consisting of one course of blocks and one course of bricks or of two brick courses, use one exterior and one interior lintel. A wall of 8-inch concrete blocks calls for two interior lintels. A 12-inch wall, consisting of three courses of brick, calls for one exterior and two interior lintels.

## An Opening in Brick Veneer

**1 Scoring the opening.** Wearing goggles and a respirator, use a circular saw fitted with a masonry blade to score the horizontal mortar joints in a saw-tooth pattern: Score joints to the first vertical joint outside each side of the marked opening. Score the bottom of the opening along a horizontal mortar joint. Score the top of the door opening along a horizontal joint and score a corresponding line on the joint 4 inches above the line for the top of the lintel. Caution: work slowly to avoid overheating the saw.

**2** **Starting the lintel channel.** At an upper corner row of the scored opening, chip through horizontal and vertical mortar joints with a 4-pound sledge hammer and a cold chisel. Remove three bricks from each of the two top courses of the lintel channel. Try not to break the bricks you remove: you will need some undamaged bricks to fill the space above the lintel.

**3** **Attaching veneer supports.** Screw a 1½-by-1½-inch angle iron into each stud behind the sheathing you have exposed. Use 2-inch wood screws and place the upper flange of the angle iron snugly against the brick above it.

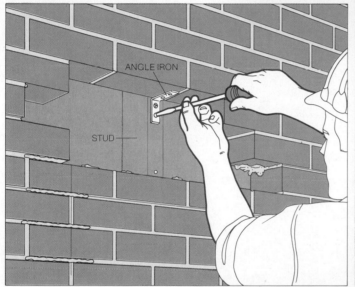

ANGLE IRON

STUD

SHOULDER

**4** **Completing the channel.** Remove the bottom course of bricks from the lintel channel, then chisel out an additional 8 inches of brick at each end of the course to make supporting surfaces, called shoulders, for the lintel.

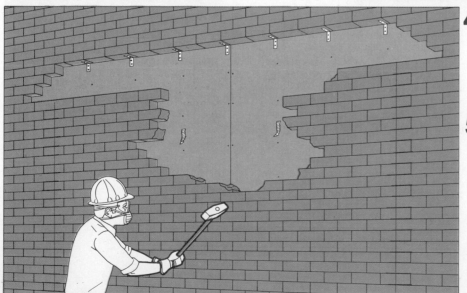

**5** **Completing the opening.** Using a 10-pound sledge hammer, smash against the center of the opening to remove most of the bricks within. As you near the edges of the opening, chisel out the remaining bricks one by one in the saw-tooth pattern scored in Step 1 (opposite).

Break several bricks in half to make bats and fill the saw-tooth pattern at one side of the opening with the bats, setting the jagged edges against the sheathing. Add ⅜ inch to the width of your door or window unit—measured to the outside of the side brickmolds—and brick in the other side with bats to create an opening of this width.

**6** **Setting the lintel.** Apply a ½-inch bed of mortar to the top of each shoulder; then, with a helper, lift the lintel into the lintel channel, with the horizontal flange on the shoulders and the vertical flange against the sheathing. Place a carpenter's level on the horizontal flange and tap the high end of the lintel into the mortar with a hammer until the lintel is level.

FLASHING

**7** **Installing the flashing.** With a heavy-duty staple gun, fasten a length of 18-mil plastic flashing to the studs between the lintel and the angle irons. Lap the flashing completely over the lintel, then cut it with a pair of scissors, leaving ½ inch of the horizontal flange exposed.

**8** **Filling in the channel.** Lay a course of bricks directly on the flashing, substituting a piece of ⅜-inch fiberboard 4 inches long for mortar in every third vertical joint between the bricks *(inset)*. When the mortar has set, pull out the pieces of fiberboard, leaving weep holes for escaping moisture. Brick in the remaining two courses, varying the thickness of the mortar beds and joints to match those at the sides of the opening. Install a rough frame *(pages 58-65)*.

FIBERBOARD

ROWLOCK COURSE

**9** **Making the sill.** Finish the bottom of the opening to match the other doors and windows in your house. If the other openings have a row of bricks on edge across the bottom, lay a matching row—called a rowlock course—across the new opening, with the back of the mortar bed about ½ inch thicker than the front, so that the bricks will slope to shed water; adjust the thickness of the bed to bring the top of the bricks to the level of the bottom of the finish unit.

Use ⅜-inch mortar joints between bricks, but adjust the joints so that you finish the course with a whole brick. Caution: the mortar must fill the joints completely to keep moisture out.

If ordinary courses—whole bricks laid lengthwise, with their narrow edges showing—form the sills for the other openings, build the new sill in the same way, adjusting the thickness of the mortar joints between courses to bring the bricks

flush with the finish unit. If the other openings have precast concrete sills, order a matching precast sill 8 inches wider than the new opening. Remove bricks at the bottom of the opening to make notches about 6 inches wide on each side, lay a bed of mortar thick enough to bring the sill flush with the finish unit and then set the precast sill in place, with its outside edge extending ½ inch beyond the face of the wall. Use bats to fill the notches at the ends of the sill.

# Supporting Solid Masonry

A wall of concrete blocks, of bricks and blocks or of solid brick, 8 to 12 inches thick and supporting the roof and upper stories of a house as well as its own considerable weight, is a formidable obstacle to a new opening, even for a professional bricklayer. Using ordinary masonry techniques, you can safely make an opening less than 40 inches wide because a natural arch rising about 3 feet up from the lintel channel will support the masonry above. But some bricks within the arch will fall out; the number depends on the strength of the mortar joints.

If your wall is old and fragile you can support the masonry with temporary shoring while you break through the wall, rather than replace 60 or 70 bricks afterward. If there are joists less than 3 feet above the opening or if you make an opening wider than 40 inches—for a sliding glass door, perhaps, or a picture window—then you must put in the shoring.

The temporary supports, called needles, are 4-by-4 beams that pierce the wall every 3 feet above the lintel channel; the needles are supported by posts inside and outside the house (Steps 1-4). As you make the opening, small natural arches form between the needles and only a few bricks will fall out. If there are joists within 3 feet of the needles, you must support them with a temporary partition inside the house (page 60).

Even with these techniques, seek professional advice before you tackle an opening that is above the ground floor, more than 10 feet wide, or within 4 feet of a corner or 2 feet of the roof.

Except for walls of 8-inch concrete block, solid-masonry walls are composed of two or three independent brick or block walls, called wythes, separated by vertical layers of mortar called collar joints. The wythes are linked by metal masonry ties embedded in the mortar or by header bricks laid across two wythes. Remove the bricks of each wythe one by one, to avoid weakening the wall with the blows of a heavy sledge hammer. When you replace the bricks, you must also replace the ties or header bricks.

The outer wythe, which merely braces the wall, requires the same type of exterior lintel as the brick veneer of a frame house; the inner wythes, which support

the roof and any joists, need a heavier interior lintel (chart, page 66).

Precast concrete lintels are often used for small openings in walls of 8-inch block—but you would need a crane to lift a long concrete lintel. Instead, install two L-shaped steel lintels, cover the vertical flanges with courses of 4-inch block (page 72, bottom right) and resume the courses of 8-inch block above the lintel.

## Post-and-Beam Shoring

**1** **Inserting the needles.** With a large cold chisel and a 3-pound sledge hammer, remove brick or block to make holes through the wall about 4 inches above the line for the top of the lintels; space the holes 3 feet apart. From outside the house, push an 8-foot length of 4-by-4—the needle—halfway through each of the holes. Inside the house, nail a double bottom plate—two 2-by-4s 3 feet longer than the width of the opening—to the floor under the ends of the needles. Outside, set a 2-foot 2-by-8 under the end of each needle.

**2** **Leveling the needles.** Cut two 4-by-4 posts to fit snugly between a needle and the plank or plate below, have helpers inside and outside the house set the posts under the needle about 6 inches from each end and check the needle with a carpenter's level. Have the helper at the lower end of the needle drive large shim shingles beneath it until the needle is level, then have both helpers simultaneously drive shingles under the posts until the top of the needle is tight against the masonry it will support. Toenail the outside post to the plank beneath it.

Set posts beneath the other needles and level each of them in the same way.

**3** **Bracing the outside posts.** With 16-penny nails, fasten two 2-by-4 braces, each 10 feet long, to the top of each outside post—the first brace at right angles to the wall, the second parallel to it—and drive 2-by-4 stakes 2 feet long at the lower end of each brace. Plumb the posts one at a time: check a face parallel to the wall with a carpenter's level, tap the top of the post with a 3-pound sledge hammer until the post is plumb and have a helper nail the first brace to its stake. Check and plumb an adjoining face of the post, then have your helper nail the second brace.

Cut ½-inch plywood cleats measuring about 8 by 4 inches, and fasten the top of each post to its needle with a cleat on each side (*inset*).

PLYWOOD CLEATS

2-BY-4 BRACES

**4** **Bracing the inside posts.** Inside the house, tap the top of each post toward or away from the wall until the post is plumb and fasten it to the needle with cleats (*above*). One by one, plumb and brace the posts in the other direction: rest one end of an 8-foot 2-by-4 on the floor against the bottom plate and nail the other end to the top of the post. Check a face of the post at right angles to the wall with a level and tap the bottom of the post along the bottom plate until the post is plumb. Make sure the shims between the post and the bottom plate are still tight, then toenail the post and shims to the bottom plate and nail the brace to the side of the plate.

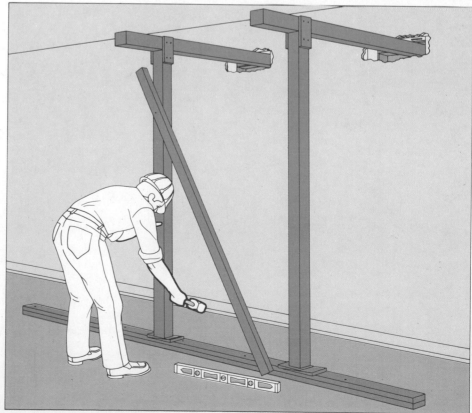

**5** **Supporting the floor.** If there is a basement or crawl space below the wall you are opening, shore the joists below the needles. For joists that run at right angles to the wall, set 2-foot pieces of 2-by-8 plank on the floor of the basement beneath the needle posts, have a helper hold a 4-by-6 beam against the joists directly beneath the bottom plate of the needles, and set 4-by-4 posts between the planks and the beam. Plumb each 4-by-4 in both directions, shim it tight to the beam and toenail it to the plank and the beam.

If the joists run parallel to the wall, shim 4-by-4 posts in place tight against the subfloor or joist directly beneath the needle posts.

## Steel Lintels and Wooden Frame

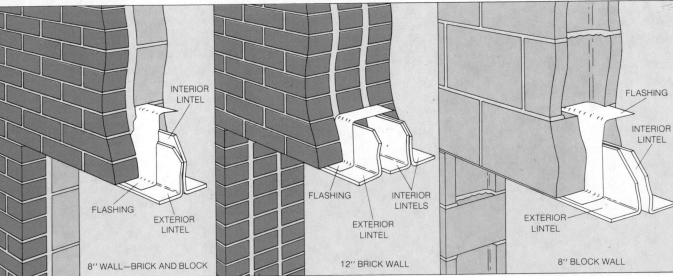

8" WALL—BRICK AND BLOCK

12" BRICK WALL

8" BLOCK WALL

**Setting the lintels.** Score the mortar joints on the outside and inside of the wall (*page 66, Step 1*) and remove the bricks or blocks one by one with a cold chisel. At the lintel channel, make shoulders for the lintels (*page 67, Step 4*). If your wall contains concrete block, stuff newspaper into the cores of the shoulder blocks and

fill the cores with mortar or build up the shoulders with courses of concrete brick. Lay a ⅜-inch mortar bed on the shoulders of the opening and, with one helper for every 5 feet of lintel, lift the lintels onto the shoulders, starting with the innermost lintel. For an 8-inch wall of bricks and concrete blocks (*left*) or an 8-inch solid brick wall,

use one interior and one exterior lintel, back to back. For a 12-inch solid-brick wall (*center*), install two interior lintels back to back, level them and fill in the brick above them, then install an exterior lintel. For an 8-inch block wall (*right*), use two interior lintels, with a course of 3-inch block beside the vertical flanges.

**Leveling the lintels.** Have a helper hold a carpenter's level on the horizontal flange of the outer lintel while you tap the high end of the lintel down into the mortar bed until the lintel is level; then line up the inner lintel or lintels with the outer one. If a lintel is too low, spread fresh mortar under it. If the lintels squeeze all of the mortar out from beneath them, support and level them with sharply angled wooden wedges; re-move the wedges when the mortar has set and patch the marks they leave.

Brick in the interior of the wall to the top of the vertical lintel flange, adjusting the mortar joints so that the courses line up with the brickwork around the opening. Spread mortar on the course above the flange, lay 18-mil plastic flashing *(opposite, bottom)* halfway across this course, and continue the courses of interior brick. Run the flashing down over the exterior lintel and cut it ½ inch from the edge of the horizontal flange. Brick up the exterior of the wall over the flashing. Remove the needles and brick in the needle holes.

Add ⅜ inch to the outside width of your door or window unit and brick in the opening to this dimension. Install a threshold *(page 69, Step 9)*.

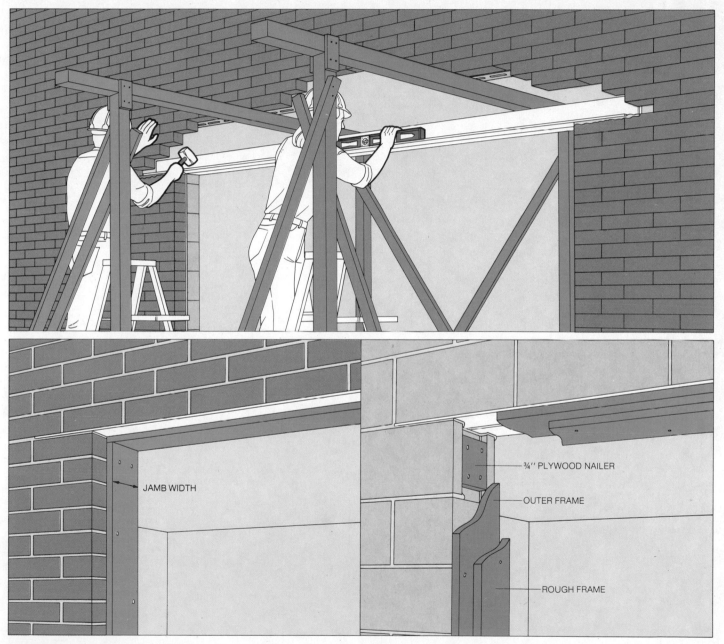

JAMB WIDTH

¾'' PLYWOOD NAILER

OUTER FRAME

ROUGH FRAME

**Installing the rough frame.** For an 8-inch brick-and-block wall or a solid-brick wall *(left)*, measure the width of the new door or window jamb, subtract ¼ inch and cut 1-inch lumber to this width. For a door, assemble a three-sided rough frame to fit snugly against the lintel and the sides of the opening; for a window, assemble a four-sided frame. Set the frame in the opening with its inner edge flush with the surface of the interior wall; hold a level against the edge of each side piece, plumb it and fasten it in place with cut masonry nails.

For an 8-inch block wall *(right)*, nail pieces of ¾-inch plywood, 3 inches square, into the U-shaped cores of the blocks on each side of the opening with cut nails. Assemble an outer frame from 1-inch lumber as wide as the block, set it in the opening and nail it to the plywood and the block with cut nails. Build a rough frame as you would for a brick wall, ¼ inch narrower than the jambs of the finish unit, set it flush with the surface of the interior wall, plumb it and nail it to the outer frame with galvanized nails.

# 3

# A Wealth of Windows

According to master architect Le Corbusier, the history of architecture is largely the history of the window. In turn, the history of the window is largely the history of changes in technology and economics. Since the 18th Century, large casement and double-hung windows have been dominant features of fine homes; by the mid-20th Century, windows had taken over a major portion of the house. While few people opted for all-glass houses like the one architect Philip Johnson built for himself in Connecticut, floor-to-ceiling window walls *(pages 92-95)* and view-framing picture windows *(pages 88-91)* became familiar features on suburban streets across America. Much of this glazing was fixed—air conditioning seemed to end the need for windows that opened to let in breezes.

This trend toward ever-larger expanses of glass may be threatened by jumps in fuel costs for both heating and air conditioning. A window is sealed only by glass, and glass is a poor insulator—1 square foot conducts as much heat as 10 square feet of wall.

Fortunately, window heat losses can be reduced, at least in some measure, when installing new windows or replacing old ones. Either job is simplified by modern windows, which are prefabricated, complete with glazing, weather stripping and operating mechanisms; they need only be positioned in a rough frame and trimmed.

The use of double glazing—two layers of glass sealed together with an air space between—can reduce heat conduction through the glass by as much as 50 per cent, and such glazing is consequently being used more widely, particularly for fixed windows. Increasingly, too, movable sashes are being installed instead of fixed glass. The sash material is also important; wood is a better insulator than metal, but a metal sash can be as economical of energy if you get the type that incorporates extra insulation.

Windows well insulated in both sash material and glazing are desirable in any climate. But the type of window to choose may depend on where you live. Where winters are harsh or where air conditioning is essential in summer, the preferred type is double-hung—its sliding sashes seal more tightly when closed than do the swinging sashes of the casement type. But in some regions, the extra breezes caught by a casement window—the entire window swings out to act as a scoop for moving air—may be an advantage.

The concern for energy is also prompting a return to old-fashioned measures for protecting windows from cold winds in winter and hot sun in summer: exterior blinds, conifer windbreaks, deciduous shade trees, overhanging eaves and awnings. By capitalizing on new materials and old techniques, the attractiveness of large multiple windows can be saved even for an energy-conscious age.

# A Factory-made Unit, Complete with All Its Parts

In some ways, adding a new window to a room is like hanging a painting or print: it can offer a pleasing view, decorate an empty wall or brighten a drab area. Of course, a window can do more, too: it can let fresh air into the house.

Once you have cut and framed a rough opening *(pages 56-73)*, installing such a window takes only a few hours—thanks to prefabricated, or prehung, units. A prehung window comes complete with the sashes, jambs and sill, and with the hardware needed to open and lock the sashes. Prehungs come in a variety of sizes and shapes, and in all of the four basic window styles: double-hung, casement, awning and sliding *(pages 8-9)*. Many have such features as a removable sash for easy cleaning, a snap-in storm window for winter and a screen for summer; some have plastic-coated weatherproof sashes and exterior trim.

In addition to these built-in conveniences, you have a choice of materials—wood, steel or aluminum. Each has advantages and disadvantages. A wooden window is traditional and elegant but it needs more upkeep than a steel or aluminum unit. Metal windows are almost maintenance-free, but they are poor insulators unless the manufacturer separates their interior and exterior parts with specially fitted insulating material.

If you simply want to replace a window, not add one, you have still another choice: a metal replacement window, consisting of a metal window frame and sashes designed to fit within the jambs and sill of a wooden window that has been stripped of its sashes, stops and balances. Metal replacement windows generally come in kit form; follow the manufacturer's instructions.

Before deciding on any window unit,

refer to manufacturers' catalogues at a building-supply store. Note the rough opening sizes required for the prehung windows you are considering, and check them against your available space. (If your space permits, always get a window large enough to double as an emergency exit.) Check for the availability of double or triple glazing and find out whether jamb extensions, helpful for fitting a shallow jamb to a deep wall *(page 78, Step 4)*, are included. When ordering casement or awning units, specify the direction in which the sashes must swing.

One final caution: Some prehung windows are assembled for use in new construction but others are designed for new or reframed openings in existing walls. The installation techniques shown on the following pages apply to the second category alone; do not use them with a unit meant for new construction.

## Fitting and Flashing

**1 Squaring the corners.** Set the window unit on a flat surface with the exterior casing—called a brickmold—down, and hold a steel square at the corners of the side jambs, head jamb and sill. If these corners are not right angles, clamp the unit to a workbench and push gently against the jamb corners to square it. Turn the unit over, and nail a temporary 1-by-2 brace diagonally between the head brickmold and a side brickmold, allowing ½ inch at the top for the drip cap *(opposite, Step 3)*; nail another brace between the sill and the other side brickmold.

**2** **Adjusting for wall thickness.** Tilt the window into the rough opening and push it back until the brickmold lies flat against the sheathing or, in a masonry wall, against the rough frame. If the jambs jut into the room, adjust with filler strips. Push the window out from inside the house until the jambs align with the interior wall. Measure the gap between the back of the brickmold and the sheathing or rough frame. Remove the window from the opening and cut wood filler strips to the lengths of the side and head jambs, making each strip as thick as the gap and as wide as the back of the brickmold. Set the strips against the back of the brickmold and nail them to the jambs with fourpenny nails.

If the jambs are not wide enough to reach the interior wall, you will need jamb extensions rather than filler strips; see page 78, Step 4.

## Fastening the Unit into the Wall

HEADER

DRIP CAP

JACK STUD

**1** **Leveling.** Outside the house, center the unit between the jack studs and, with a helper, lift it until the head brickmold fits beneath the drip cap, and the tops of the side jambs butt against the header. Use a carpenter's level to find which top corner of the window is lower than the other. Anchor this corner with an eightpenny finishing nail driven through the brickmold into the header. Lower the other corner to level the head brickmold and nail that corner to the header.

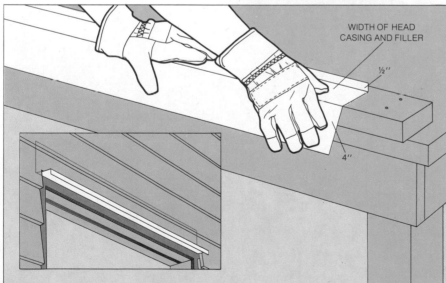

WIDTH OF HEAD CASING AND FILLER

½″

4″

**3** **Providing a drip cap.** For a wall with siding, cut a strip of aluminum flashing as long as the exterior head casing and 4½ inches wider than the combined thickness of the brickmold and any filler strips. With an awl, scribe a line on the flashing ½ inch from a long edge, then bend the section over a 2-by-4 to a 90° angle at the score line. Turn the flashing over, scribe a second line 4 inches from the other long edge and make a bend in the opposite direction. Insert the 4-inch section between the siding and the sheathing at the top of the window opening *(inset)*.

You need not make a drip cap for a masonry wall. Because the window is recessed in the masonry and flat against the rough frame, rain flowing down the wall will not run onto it.

**2 Shimming the window.** Inside the house, check to be sure that the head jamb is level; then, while a helper outside the house holds the window flush against the sheathing, insert shims between the finish sill and the rough sill. Drive eightpenny finishing nails down through the finish sill and the shims below it into the rough sill. Finally, insert at least two pairs of shims between the side jambs and jack studs on each side of the window frame, and fill the gaps between the jambs and studs with insulation. Caution: do not insert shims thicker than the space between the jambs and jack studs—larger shims can bow the jambs.

If a metal window unit fits the rough frame exactly, it does not have to be shimmed. In this case, simply fasten the window directly to the rough frame, using 1-inch flathead wood screws driven through the predrilled holes in the jambs and the finish sill (*inset*).

**3 Securing the brickmold.** Outside the house, fasten the casing to the rough frame with eight-penny nails at 12-inch intervals. Countersink the nails and fill all the holes with wood putty.

Wearing gloves, push the drip cap tightly over the edge of the head brickmold. Run silicone or butyl caulking along the joints where the drip cap and side brickmold meet the siding.

ROUGH
SILL

FINISH
SILL

JAMB EXTENSIONS

**4 Adjusting the depth of the jambs.** If the jambs of the installed window do not reach the face of the wall inside the house, glue and nail strips of wood called jamb extensions to the inner edges of the jambs. Your prehung window may come with jamb extensions; if so, fasten them to the jambs, and plane their outer edges flush to the face of the wall with a block plane. If you do not have jamb extensions, you can make your own: cut ¾-inch wood strips to the lengths of the jambs and to the required thickness, fasten them sawed side out and smooth the rough edges with sandpaper.

# A Choice of Shapes

Prehung windows are made not only in the conventional rectangular form but in odd shapes that can fit into the most limited and unlikely spaces, such as cramped stair wells and shallow attics. These windows generally have fixed rather than movable sashes and cannot be used for ventilation, but they do bring light to dark spaces and their configurations give them unexpected charm or traditional elegance. Some are circles, half circles or quarter circles. Others, like the fanlight of a period door, are shaped like part of an ellipse. Still others—diamonds, octagons and the like—have straight jambs, but no right angles.

Because of their shapes, these windows call for special steps in installation: for example, the opening for a curved window is cut before the rough framing is assembled, the reverse of the conventional sequence. The methods vary from one window shape to another. The opening for a circular window can be plotted with a string compass (right, Step 1), but the straight sides of half or quarter circles must be leveled or plumbed, and the shape of an oval window is best traced on a wall from the window frame itself (page 81, bottom). Circular windows are braced differently from oval ones; windows with straight jambs are braced by a third system.

There is one feature, though, that most odd-shaped windows have in common: virtually all of them need jamb extensions (page 81, Step 6) to fit them to a wall. In many models the shapes of these extensions make them impractical for an amateur to fashion; order them as accessories when you get the window unit.

**2** **Installing the braces.** Measure the diameter of the window at the outer edges of the jamb, multiply the measurement by 0.4, then mark and cut four 2-by-4 braces to this length, beveling their ends in from the marks at a 45° angle. Toenail the braces to the jack studs, header and rough sill to form an equal-sided octagon.

## Putting In a Round Window

**1** **Making the opening.** From inside the house, drill through sheathing and siding to mark the window center. Outside, center a string compass—a length of string with a nail at one end and a pencil at the other—at the hole and draw a circle to the diameter of the outer edges of the brickmold. Drill a starter hole on the circle and, using a saber saw with a 4-inch blade, cut the circle out of the siding and sheathing. If the sheathing is plywood, save the cutout disk for later use (page 80, Step 3). Install a rough frame of jack studs, a header and a rough sill (pages 58-65) projecting 1 inch into the cutout opening.

**3** **Cutting the sheathing ring.** Using a string compass *(page 79, Step 1)*, draw a circle within the cutout disk of sheathing, making the diameter equal to the outer diameter of the window jamb; clamp the disk over the edge of a workbench, turning it as necessary, to cut out a ring. Outside the house, fit the ring into the opening and fasten it to the rough frame and braces with fourpenny nails. Caulk the gap between the ring and the sheathing around it.

If the house has board rather than plywood sheathing, cut the ring from exterior plywood of the same thickness as the sheathing.

WIDTH OF EXTERIOR CASING

4″

**4** **Flashing the window.** Wearing gloves, cut a strip of flashing 4 inches wider than the outer edge of the casing and as long as half the circumference of the casing; cut tabs 4 inches long at 1-inch intervals *(inset)*. Bend the tabbed part of the strip to a right angle *(page 77, Step 3)* and shape the untabbed section to a semicircle around the casing. Outside the house, insert the tabbed section of the strip between the siding and the sheathing at the top of the opening.

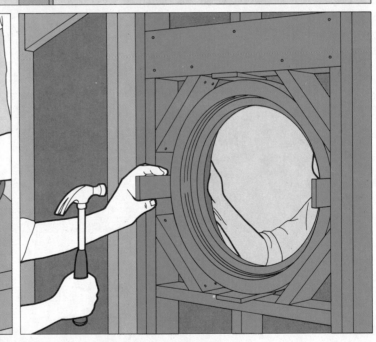

**5** **Shimming and fastening the window.** Have a helper outside the house hold the window in the opening, with the back of the casing set firmly against the sheathing. Inside the house, drive eight shims between the jamb and the framing parts around it, in the following sequence: one at the rough sill, one at the header, one at each jack stud and four at the braces.

Outside the house, fasten the casing to the sheathing and frame with eightpenny nails at 8-inch intervals. Inside the house, score the protruding ends of the shims and break them off; outside, caulk above the flashing and at the joint between the casing and the siding.

**6 Finishing off the window.** Glue jamb extensions, purchased with the window, to the edges of the jamb, and anchor each with two countersunk flathead screws. Put up the finish-wall material. Using a block plane (*pages 20-22*), trim the jamb extensions flush with the face of the wall. Nail the interior casing, supplied by the manufacturer, to the jamb extensions.

JAMB EXTENSIONS

## Fanlights and Ovals

**1 Locating the window.** Inside the house (*right, top*), set the casing of the window against the exposed sheathing at the location you have chosen—use a level to be sure the finish sill is horizontal—and mark and drill pilot holes through the sheathing and siding at the points where the casing meets the sill. Outside the house (*right, bottom*), set the casing against the siding, using the pilot holes to position the window. Recheck the sill to see that it is still level and trace the outline of the casing and sill on the siding. Cut the traced opening through the siding and sheathing (*page 62, Step 1*).

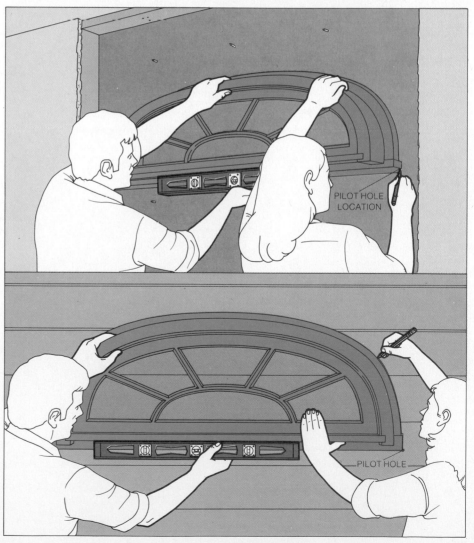

PILOT HOLE LOCATION

PILOT HOLE

**2 Making a sheathing insert.** Center the window, jamb side down, on the cutout piece of sheathing and trace the outline of the jamb and finish sill. With a saber saw, cut through the sheathing along the outline.

Build a rough frame *(pages 58-65)*, with the header, jack studs and rough sill projecting 1 inch into the cutout opening.

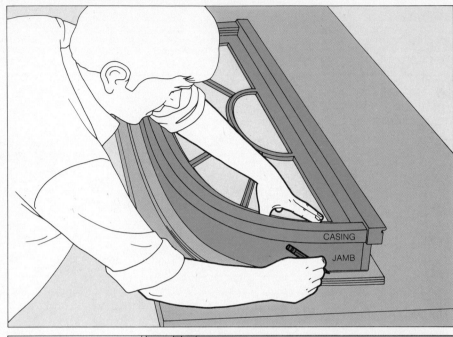

## A Rough Frame for a Diamond

**Anatomy of a special frame.** The window below is fastened to diagonal 2-by-4 braces rather than to the frame. The rough frame *(pages 58-65)* is 1 inch taller and wider than the window; the braces, marked like those in Step 3, run to the exact midpoint of each side of the rough frame. Each of the four window jambs is shimmed at two points, and outside the house the window unit is nailed to the diagonal braces through the brickmold on each side.

**3 Making the braces.** While a helper outside the house holds the window unit against the framing of the opening, work inside the house to set lengths of 2-by-4 diagonally against the header and the jack studs, ½ inch from the window jamb. Mark the 2-by-4s for braces at the points where they intersect the header and the jack studs. Cut the ends of the braces at 45° angles and, after the window has been removed from the opening, toenail the braces to the header and the jack studs. Then nail and caulk the sheathing insert, and go on to install the window unit as you would a circular model *(pages 79-81)*.

# Graceful Bays and Bows

A wide bay window or a bow window serves two purposes: it floods a room with light, and it adds space for a seat or a window garden. Both types are available prefabricated. Bay windows, the more common kind, range from 5 to 9 feet wide in 1-foot increments; most have a fixed center window parallel to the wall and two side windows set at an angle. In a bow window the angle between sections is gentler and the unit as a whole takes the shape of a graceful curve; these relatively expensive windows come in 5- to 11-foot widths.

The kits for both bay and bow windows generally include the windows; a head, or ceiling, board; a window seat; and, in many models, an insulating panel below the seat. Some units come with ornamental support brackets called knee braces, which fit beneath the window; for others you may have to make wooden braces yourself according to the manufacturer's instructions, or have an iron shop fabricate metal ones for you.

Bay and bow windows are installed in much the same way. Prepare the rough opening as you would for an ordinary prehung unit *(Chapter 2)*, but consider the manufacturer's instructions before trimming back the siding from the sheathing *(page 62, Step 2):* unlike standard windows, some bay and bow units are designed to rest against the face of the siding rather than on the sheathing.

For a window under a roof overhang, cut the opening so the top of the window unit will rest against the soffit when the unit is installed. If the window will have no overhang directly above it, you will need to put on a roof.

Many units are available with roof kits *(pages 85-86, Steps 1-4),* consisting of a wooden drip cap, precut end and intermediate rafters, thicker hip rafters, and plywood sheathing cut to fit over the rafters. Most roof kits do not include shingles or flashing, but once installed, they can be flashed and shingled like any other roof. Some units can be purchased with prefabricated metal roofs. A few manufacturers do not provide a roof: you will have to build your own.

Bay and bow windows are bulky and heavy; do not attempt to install one without helpers to lift the unit into the opening and to steady it on sawhorses while you nail it to the rough frame.

## Attaching a Bay Window

**1** **Setting the window in the opening.** With one helper for every 3 feet of window span, lift the unit into place. First rest the bottom of the insulating panel on the sill, then tilt the window up and into the opening until the brickmold butts against the exposed sheathing. Center the unit between the jack studs and brace it every 3 feet with sawhorses.

**2** **Leveling the seat board.** Inside the house use a mason's level to find the higher end of the seat and nail that end into the rough sill, 2 inches from the end jamb. Shim between the insulating panel and the rough sill until the other end is level and nail it in place the same way. Because of their weight, windows 8 feet wide or wider should be shimmed with thin pieces of slate roofing shingle rather than with wood.

**3** **Plumbing the jambs.** Hold a carpenter's level first against the edge and then against the side of each end jamb, have helpers move the window slightly from outside the house until the jamb is plumb, then install shims 1 foot apart between the jamb and the jack stud. Wooden shims serve for this purpose. Drive nails through the jamb and shims into the stud, taking special care to avoid driving a nail through the balancing mechanism of a double-hung window.

END JAMB

**4** **Anchoring the headboard.** Hammer a wooden shim every 8 inches between the headboard and the header, then nail through the headboard and shims into the header.

Fill all gaps between the window unit and the rough frame with insulation.

HEADER

HEADBOARD

**5** **Fastening the knee brackets.** Outside the house, set a knee bracket—one from the kit or one you make—under each mullion, with the long leg of the bracket against the siding; drill pilot holes through the bracket into the cripple stud within the wall. If there is no cripple stud directly in line with the mullion, toenail one between the sole plate and rough sill. Fasten the bracket to the stud with ⅜-inch lag bolts, then fasten the short leg to the insulating panel of the unit with a wood screw.

Caulk the joints between the window and the siding of the house. Nail 1-inch quarter-round molding under the window along the joint between the insulating panel and the siding.

## Adding a Precut Roof

**1** **Marking the siding.** Nail the wooden drip cap supplied by the manufacturer to the trim at the top of the window, then place the three pieces of roof sheathing from the kit against the drip cap and the siding, with the edges of the triangular end pieces overlapping the center piece. Mark the outline of the roof on the siding and remove the roof sheathing; saw the siding along the marks (*page 62, Step 2*) and pry it off.

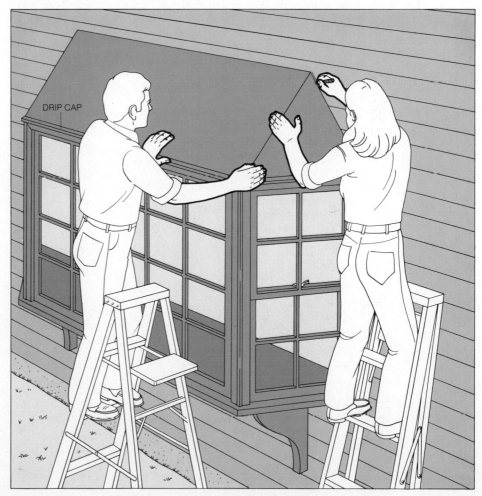

**2** **Strapping the window to the house.** About 10 inches above the top of the window, fasten a length of perforated metal strap to the wall stud behind each corner of the window, using a lag bolt and washer. Pull the strap down to the window corner and fasten it to the top of the mullion post there with a lag bolt.

**3** **Installing the rafters.** Attach a hip rafter—thicker than the other rafter pieces in the kit—above each mullion, placing it between the drip cap and the point where the horizontal and vertical cuts in the house siding meet (*below, left*). Toenail the rafter to the sheathing and the headboard. Attach one of the other rafters flat against the house wall at each end, nailing it to the drip cap, the hip rafter and the sheathing (*below, right*). Nail the remaining rafters to the headboard and to the sheathing, spacing them at equal intervals between the hip rafters.

HEADBOARD

HIP RAFTER — END RAFTER

**4** **Sheathing the roof.** Place each piece of triangular sheathing completely over the end rafter and halfway over the hip rafter, and nail it to the rafters at 6-inch intervals. Set batts of insulation on the headboard and against the triangular pieces. Place the center piece over the hip rafters and the drip cap; nail it to the rafters.

If your roof kit contains fascia boards to cover the ends of the rafters, place each one tight against the underside of the sheathing and then nail the board to the rafters.

**5** **Weatherproofing the roof.** Nail a preformed metal drip edge tight against the edge of each piece of roof sheathing with roofing nails, but do not install the other metal flashing as yet. Nail asphalt-impregnated roofing felt over each piece of sheathing and trim away excess felt with a utility knife. Working from the drip edge up, nail shingles to each face of the roof—but do not apply shingles to the hip ridge.

**6** **Flashing the sides.** Pry the pieces of siding just above the roof slightly away from the sheathing. Working from the bottom of the roof, slip pieces of flashing bent at a right angle beneath each course of shingles and between the sheathing and the siding of the house. Lap each successive piece over the one below it and nail the upper end to the roof; the next piece of flashing will cover the nail. Renail the siding.

DRIP EDGE

**7** **Flashing the top.** Bend flashing 8 inches longer than the length of the middle piece of roof sheathing lengthwise into a right angle and notch the corners to fit under the siding at each end. Slide one edge under the siding, spread roofing cement on the shingles at the roof top and press the lower edge of the flashing into the cement. Bend the notched projections over the hips and seal all edges with roofing cement.

To complete the roofing job, secure hip shingles over each hip ridge with nails.

# Capturing a View with a Picture Window

Most people consider any large window a picture window, but that term properly applies only if the opening serves as a picture on the wall—a frame for an attractive scene outdoors. You can buy ready-to-install picture windows, but if you build your own window you can make it frame a view just as a picture frame does a painting. The scene that appears on your wall then includes only what you want in the picture, as do the custom-made examples on pages 96A-96G.

While some striking picture windows are small, most are large and, like a landscape painting, wider than they are tall. The size leads to considerable heat loss in winter (and heat gain in summer), making double-pane insulating glass advisable, if it is available in the size you require; otherwise you may want to alter the dimensions of your window to match standard glass sizes. And because such a large, heavy sheet of glass is required, it is best installed by a professional glazier.

The window frame, which resembles that of a standard window except that it does not have a movable sash, fits into a standard rough frame (Chapter 2). It requires rabbet and dado joints, but because there are only a few they are most conveniently made by hand with a chisel rather than with a router. Since the wood surfaces will show, the parts should be made of the knotless, kiln-dried pine often called shop lumber, which has its thicknesses designated in a special way, as so many quarters of an inch. Thus a shop-lumber 2-by-6 would be designated 8/4-by-6. Make the jambs of 5/4 or 6/4 stock, as wide as the thickness of the wall; use 8/4-by-8 stock for the sill.

The glazier will provide exterior stops; determine their thickness from him and make your interior stops the same size—at least ½ inch thick for single-pane glass, ¾ inch for insulating glass. Buy brickmold, or exterior casing, wide enough to span the gap between the finish frame and the studs and header of the rough opening; order enough interior casing for all four sides of the frame.

On a frame for insulating glass, the inside dimensions must be ½ inch greater in height and width than the glass itself, so that the glass can float in the glazing compound; for single-pane installation, allow ¼ inch for clearance. And for a good paint seal, both the brickmold and exterior stops should be set ⅛ inch back from, not flush with, the jamb edges.

**The parts of a picture window.** In this frame, the head jamb is seated in grooves, called dadoes, at the tops of the side jambs. At their bottoms, notches, called rabbets, hold a single sill, its exterior portion sloping downward to shed water. Strips of brickmold, mitered at the corners, are fastened to the outer edges of the head and side jambs and rest on the horns of the sill. The glass is set against interior stops, then sealed on the outside and secured with exterior stops. After the glass is installed, mitered interior casing covers the frame on all four sides.

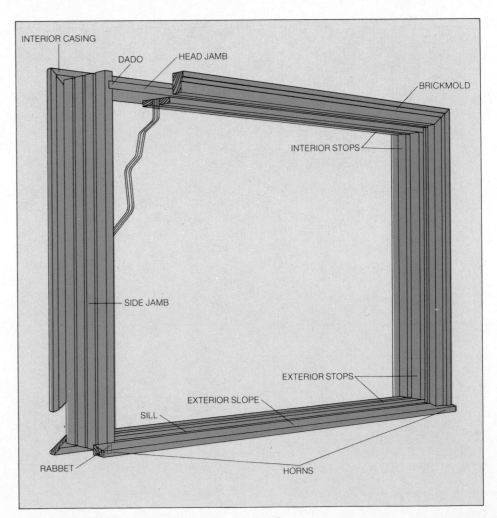

## Assembling a Finish Frame

**1 Marking dadoes and rabbets.** Using a combination square and a utility knife, mark the thickness of the sill stock across the ends of both side jambs. From this rabbet line, measure up and mark the inside height of the frame for the bottom of the dadoes; then, at a distance equal to the thickness of the head jamb, mark a second line above for the top of the dadoes. Set a marking gauge at ½ inch and follow the procedures on page 117, Step 2, to mark the gain, or depth, of the rabbets and dadoes.

Cut the side jambs 1 inch above the dado marks. Then go on to cut the head jamb to the inside width of the frame plus 1 inch for the combined depth of the dadoes.

**2 Cutting the joints.** Saw along the waste side of the rabbet line, cutting across the board evenly down to the gain mark. Do the same for the dadoes, but make two or three additional cuts within the area to be chiseled.

**3 Chiseling out the rabbet.** Drive a 1½-inch wood chisel, beveled edge up, into the end of the jamb stock at the gain mark, all the way to the saw cut, and split out the waste wood. To finish the rabbet, hold the chisel with its beveled side up in one hand and guide the blade with the other hand to smooth the rough surface *(inset)*.

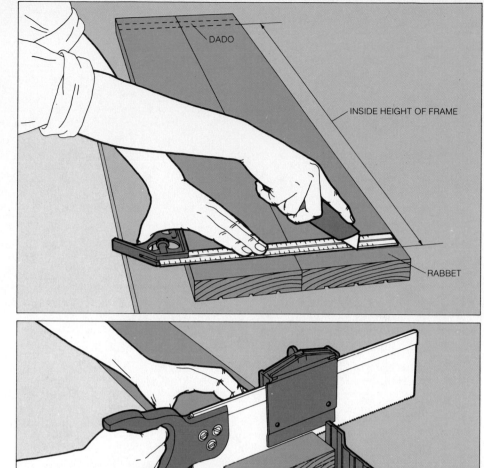

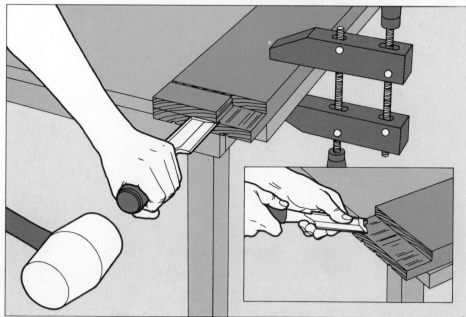

**4 Chiseling out the dado.** Working from each side of the jamb toward the middle, drive a 1-inch chisel, beveled side down, into the edge of the jamb just above the gain mark for the dado. Smooth the groove, using the chisel bevel side up, as on page 89, Step 3.

**5 Grooving the sill stock.** Saw along the underside of the sill stock to make three parallel grooves, ¼ inch deep and as wide as the saw blade; run the grooves ½, 3½ and 6½ inches in from the exterior edge of the stock. Then trim the grooved sill to a length ¼ inch more than the inside width of the window frame plus twice the width of the brickmold.

**6 Making the horns.** Across each end of the sill, draw a line at a distance from the sill end equal to ⅜ inch less than the width of the brickmold. Measure from the interior edge of the sill along this line a distance equal to the width of the jamb stock, and draw a perpendicular line from this point to the end of the sill. Cut along these lines to form the sill horns.

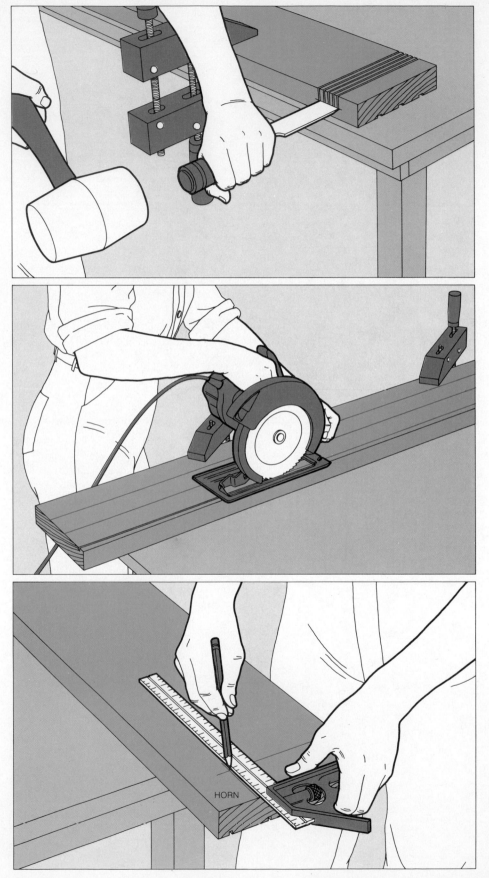

HORN

**7 Setting the slope of the sill.** Hold a T bevel set at a 15° angle on the end of each horn and draw a line from the inside corner of the horn down to its exterior edge. Connect both ends of these lines with horizontal lines *(inset)* and plane the sill to these marks *(page 121, Step 5)*.

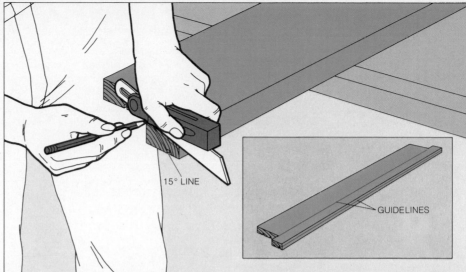

15° LINE

GUIDELINES

**8 Assembling the pieces.** Insert the head jamb you cut in Step 1 into the dadoes on the side jambs, then insert the sill, exterior edge up, into the rabbets and nail the parts together. Use eightpenny galvanized nails, driving them through the side jambs. Turn the frame over and, with the exterior part of the sill projecting beyond the bench, square and brace the corners of the frame as described on page 76, Step 1.

Attach the brickmold following the procedure for interior casings *(pages 29-31, Steps 1-7)* with one exception: the bottom edges of the side-pieces must be mitered, front to back, at a 15° angle to match the sill slope. Apply two coats of wood preservative to the frame and nail it into the rough frame as described on pages 77-78.

**9 Installing the interior stops.** Using a combination square, mark the locations of the stops on the face of one of the side jambs. First draw a line ⅛ inch from the outside edge of the jamb for the setback of the exterior stops, then draw a line for the width of the stop. Add ¼ inch for glazing compound and an additional allowance for glass thickness, measure this total distance from the exterior-stop line and draw a line for the glass channel. Draw a line the width of the interior stop in from the glass channel and extend this line onto all four sides of the frame.

Nail the top and bottom interior stops along the line. Fit the interior side stops between the top and bottom stops: if the interior stops are rectangular, use butt joints; if they have a molded surface, cope the joint *(page 32, Step 2)*. (The exterior stops will be installed by the glazier.)

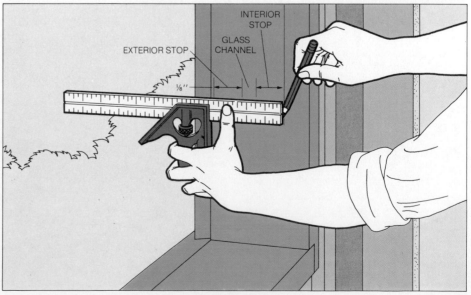

INTERIOR STOP

GLASS CHANNEL

EXTERIOR STOP

⅛''

# Bringing the Outdoors In with a Window Wall

Normally, a window fits into an opening in a wall, but in some homes the wall itself, from floor to ceiling, is a window that completely opens a room to the outdoors. Window walls are most often seen in low houses of contemporary design, but within certain limitations they can be built into or added to a home of any style. The major limitation is imposed by requirements of structural stability. Glass walls have comparatively poor resistance to the lateral pressure of high winds and few are strong enough to support the weight of a story above them. If you plan a window wall that is more than 9 feet wide, is less than 4 feet from a corner of the house or must support higher floors as well as a roof, consult an architect or a structural engineer.

In addition to structural problems, large glass areas bring weatherproofing difficulties. A wall of single-pane glass offers little protection against extremes of heat and cold outdoors, although you can fit storm windows to a completed wall or—at greater cost—build the wall with double glazing in the first place. Providing ventilation requires extra construction. The panes of a typical window wall are stationary. You can, however, install windows with movable sashes by adjusting the stud spacing and blocking height to create rough openings that will accommodate prehung casement, sliding or awning windows.

Window-wall construction begins with a braced rough opening like the one on page 58: a header resting on 2-by-4 jack studs and flanked by two 2-by-4 king studs, with the old wall studs and sole plate removed. The header, set tight against the old wall top plate, is higher than that of an ordinary window or door opening, and because it is supported by studs at intervals of 3 feet or less, a sandwich of 2-by-6s and ½-inch plywood is adequate (page 59).

Inside this opening is the frame of the window wall itself: a grid of 2-by-6s with rabbeted and dadoed joints. Since these boards will be visible in the completed wall, you may prefer to select the wood, paying extra for lumber with fewer knots than ordinary construction grade. For the studs at the middle of the wall, which consist of paired 2-by-6s, try to get

boards with perfectly square edges rather than the ordinary rounded edges, to conceal the line where two boards meet.

Use a router and jigs to cut the numerous rabbets and dadoes in the frame pieces. For the rabbets that hold the glass at the outer edges of the frame, adjust the width and depth of the cuts to the type of glass you use. Most single panes require rabbets ½ inch deep and 1 inch wide; double glazing requires rabbets ½ inch deep and 1½ inches wide. If you must cut rabbets deeper than ½ inch, use

lumber thicker than single 2-by-6s for the middle horizontal blocking, which must be rabbeted on both sides (below, inset)—3-by-6s or paired 2-by-6s will serve.

To minimize the time that the interior of your house must be exposed to the elements, cut all the rabbets and dadoes before you cut through the sheathing and siding of the old wall. Installing the glass is best done by a professional—these large panes and their precise fitting with caulking and wooden stops call for special skills and tools.

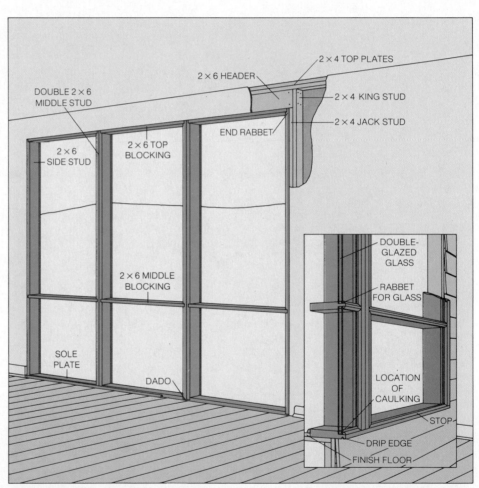

**A wall of glass.** This typical window wall consists of large panes of glass set in an interlocking grid of 2-by-6s. Above the grid, a doubled 2-by-6 header, supported by 2-by-4 jack studs, fits against the top plate of the main wall. At the bottom of the grid, a 2-by-6 sole plate rests on the subfloor. Between the header and the sole plate, 2-by-6 studs—single at the outer ends of the grid, doubled in the middle—and two rows of 2-by-6 horizontal blocking are joined with da-

do and rabbet joints to form rectangular openings for panes of glass. All the 2-by-6s of the grid project slightly beyond the siding of the house and are rabbeted at their outer edges to accept the glass—in this example, double panes for insulation (inset). The glass is sealed with caulking secured by stops nailed to the 2-by-6s. Along the bottom face of the sole plate, a shallow groove forms a drip edge to keep water from flowing back to the siding.

## Routing the Boards

**1 Cutting a drip edge.** Cut a 2-by-6 for the sole plate to fit between the jack studs and, with a router and a ¼-inch bit, cut a ¼-inch-deep groove ¼ inch from one edge along the underside of the sole plate. Guide the router with a straight board temporarily nailed to the 2-by-6.

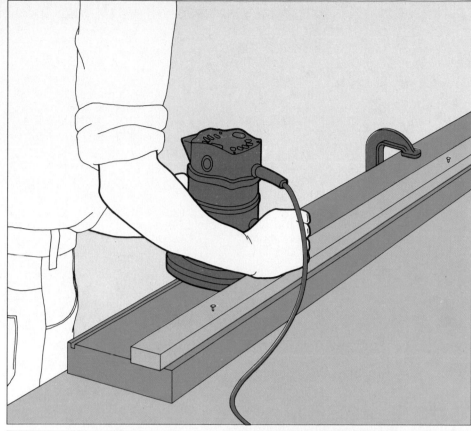

**2 Rabbeting for the glass.** Cutting a rabbet wide enough for most panes of glass—1 to 1½ inches—requires two passes of a router with a ¾-inch bit set to cut ½ inch deep, and two positions of a guide like the one used in Step 1. For a rabbet 1½ inches wide, position the guide so that the first router pass cuts a ¾-inch notch along the edge of the 2-by-6, then move the guide to widen the rabbet by another ¾ inch.

Cut rabbets along one edge of the sole plate and of all the 2-by-6s that make up the wall frame; for the blocking within the frame, rabbet both the top and bottom of the outer edge.

Cut the rabbeted 2-by-6s to length for the studs and blocking, allowing ½ inch for joints at dadoes and end rabbets *(Step 5)*. Mark the sole plate and the studs for dadoes and end rabbets: end rabbets are 1½ inches wide; dadoes are 3 inches wide in the sole plate, 1½ inches wide in each of the studs.

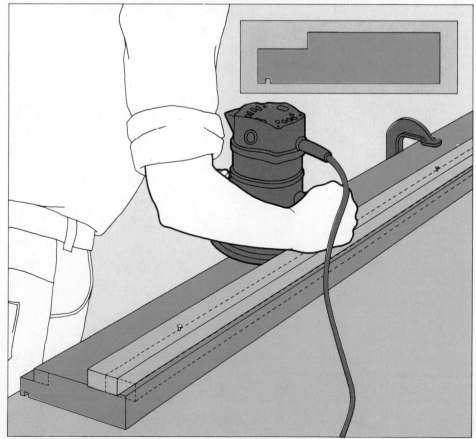

**3** **A jig for dadoes and end rabbets.** With a combination square, draw two lines straight across two 2-by-4s, separating the lines by the diameter of the router plate plus ¾ inch; then set the 2-by-4s 5½ inches apart (the width of a 2-by-6) and screw two 1-by-2s to them just outside the lines. Using a ¾-inch bit set to a depth of ½ inch, make two passes with the router to cut a notch 1½ inches wide into the edge of each 2-by-4.

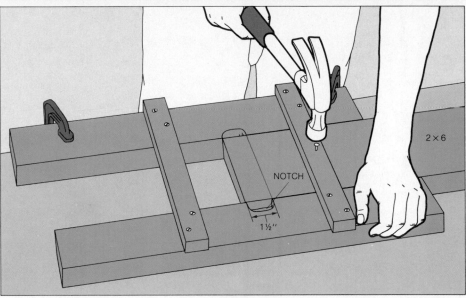

**4** **Cutting the end rabbets.** Clamp the jig to a workbench, slide the end of a stud or sole plate into it, aligning one edge of the jig notches with a line drawn to mark the width of the rabbet on the 2-by-6, and temporarily nail the jig to the 2-by-6. Set the router bit in one of the notches of the jig, start the router, push it along one of the 1-by-2s until the bit reaches the second notch; then make a second pass along the other 1-by-2. Cut rabbets at the tops of all the studs and at both ends of the 2-by-6 sole plate.

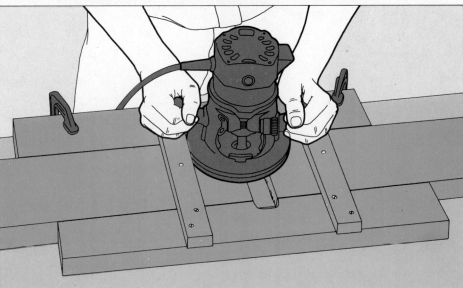

**5** **Cutting the dadoes.** Cut the dadoes in the studs as you did the end rabbets in Step 4, aligning the notches of the jig with marks for the edges of each dado. For the dadoes of the sole plate, which are 3 inches wide, move the plate 1½ inches after making the first cuts.

The pieces of the wall frame are now ready to be nailed in place. Cut away the sheathing and siding of the old wall (*page 62, Steps 1-2*).

**6** **Nailing the studs in place.** Set the sole plate on the subfloor, butted against the finish floor *(page 92, inset)*, and nail it to the subfloor; then set a stud into one of the end rabbets of the plate and nail it to the jack stud. Repeat the procedure for the stud at the other end of the wall. Nail the intermediate studs together in pairs, set them into the sole-plate dadoes and adjust them for plumb; then toenail them to the header and the sole plate.

**7** **Putting in the blocking.** Slip the top and middle blocking pieces into the rabbets and dadoes of the studs. Nail through the studs into the ends of the blocks wherever possible so that the nails are invisible; toenail only where necessary.

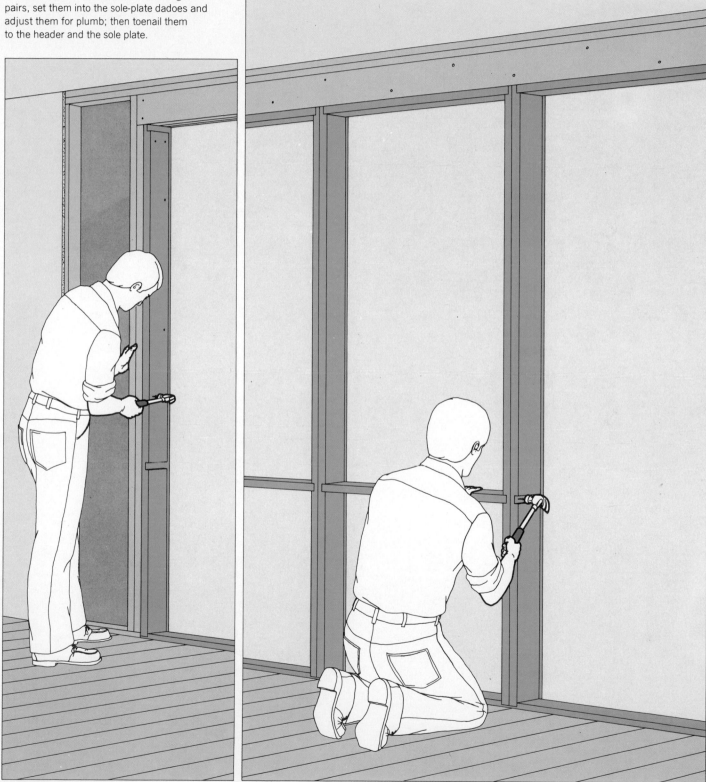

# 4

# A Door for Every Purpose

**Handcrafting a doorframe.** In the craftsman's technique of hanging a door, fine lumber chosen to blend with the decor of the house has been cut for jambs—the pieces that cover the top and sides of a wall opening and hold the door in place. At left, a recessed inset called a mortise has been outlined on the lumber and partly chiseled out; the hinge leaves will be set into finished mortises on the jamb and the door.

If you go shopping for a door these days you may be in for some surprises. Over the last decade or two, doormakers have revolutionized their product with new materials, designs and methods of manufacture. Old stereotypes—a door is always heavy, always made of wood, always installed by painstaking custom craftsmanship—no longer apply. An exterior door, for instance, is as likely to be made of metal as of wood. Metal resists damage better than wood, it lasts longer, it is fabricated more quickly and efficiently, and a traditional objection to it in an outside door—that it does not insulate as well as wood—has now been met by cores of rigid plastic insulation that make metal doors better insulators than wooden ones.

The greatest revolution of all has taken place in the form in which a door is generally delivered for installation. Traditionally, a door was installed by the most skillful carpenter in a contractor's crew. The job called for precise fitting to close tolerances, and every part but the door itself, from the jigsaw puzzle of jambs and trim work to the holes for locks and bolts, was fashioned by hand. Today, that work is done at the factory. A prefabricated—or, in the language of modern carpentry, prehung—door is shipped as a unit, with the frame assembled, the door hinged and mounted, and the lock holes cut. The entire unit, leveled and plumbed, is simply nailed into a wall opening—a job that takes, at most, a couple of hours, and one that a beginner can do almost as easily as a veteran craftsman.

The idea of the prehung has spread to every kind of door manufacture, and the range of models increases almost every year. Once designed as conventional interior and exterior doors, prehungs now come in specialized designs for special purposes. Some are features of modern home building—a sliding, floor-to-ceiling set of glass doors, for example, links a recreation room to a patio or a yard. Sectional garage doors that roll on overhead tracks can take the place of swinging doors that sagged under their own weight and dragged against the ground. And older styles are being revived as prehungs: Victorian pocket doors, which slid into a wall between dining and living rooms, now come in kits for modern houses.

Meanwhile, the craftsman's tradition of hanging a door from scratch is far from ended. For all their versatility, prehung doors do not come in every style or size, and an odd-sized opening still must be fitted with a door in the old way. An antique door, acquired for its beauty or associations, can be installed in no other way, because its frame and trim must be assembled on the spot. Such a job is a demanding one, but once the basic skills of accurate measurement and cutting are mastered and the sequence of procedures understood, it, too, becomes routine.

# Prehung Units that Make a Tough Job Easy

A prehung door unit is the woodworking equivalent of a ready-to-wear suit. The most difficult part of the work is done in a factory—the jambs are fastened together, the door is hinged and mounted, the lock holes are cut. You do the final fitting: setting the unit snugly into a new rough opening (*Chapter 2*) or an old opening formerly occupied by a door you have discarded, fastening the unit to the rough frame and—for an exterior door—adding the casing inside the house (*pages 29-31*).

The only special technique involved is a trick used to shim the jambs of a prehung door. The brickmold prevents you from driving horizontal shim shingles past each other from opposite sides of the door. You must cut off the sharp ends of the shims, then set the butt end of one shim against the brickmold and insert the blunted end of the other alongside it to adjust the thickness of the pair.

Prehung door units range from a lightweight interior door to an ornate double front door with sidelights and an overhead transom. Exterior-door units are available with a solid-core wooden door or with a steel-shell door that has an insulating plastic core. Both types of door have wooden jambs. Prehung door units generally come with weather stripping already installed and an adjustable threshold; they are available with double-glazed, shatterproof windows built into the door, or built into the jamb as a sidelight or transom.

Double-door units (*page 101*), either exterior doors or interior French doors, are hinged in the same fashion as ordinary doors, but they have special hardware and trim. The inactive door—the one that generally remains closed—is held at the top and bottom by flush bolts. To keep the active door—the one that is regularly opened and closed—from swinging past the inactive one, a strip of molding called an astragal is fastened to the edge of the inactive door.

The construction of solid-core interior door units differs from that of their exterior counterparts—there is no brickmold, so you must add casing on both sides of the jamb; the doorstop is a separate piece rather than part of the jamb; and the threshold is often omitted. But the installation techniques are virtually the same. Solid-core doors should be used wherev-er noise, security or the possible spread of fire are important considerations—in a doorway leading to the garage, for example, or for a bedroom door.

In other situations you can save both money and labor by installing a hollow-core wooden door with a split jamb (*page 102*). In these units, the casing on both sides is installed at the factory, and the two preassembled jamb sections are slipped into the rough opening from opposite sides to sandwich the wall.

In most localities you will have to order the unit from a lumberyard and wait a week or so for delivery. You must specify the width of the jamb (generally $4\frac{5}{8}$ inches for walls covered with wallboard and $5\frac{3}{8}$ inches for plaster walls) and the width of the finished door (24 inches for closets, 30 or 32 inches for other interior doors, 36 or 42 inches for exterior doors, and 60, 64 or 72 inches for double doors). You must also specify whether the door will open from the right or left and whether it will swing in or out; for a double door, specify which door will be active. And you should provide manufacturer's templates or exact specifications for the lockset (*page 103*).

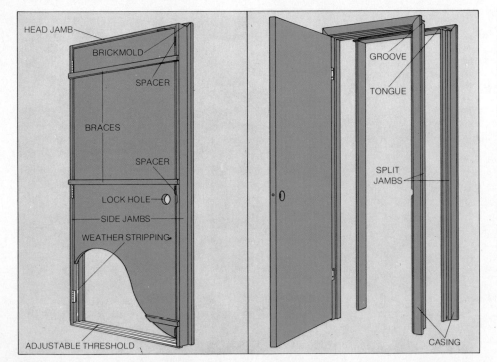

HEAD JAMB
BRICKMOLD
SPACER
BRACES
SPACER
LOCK HOLE
SIDE JAMBS
WEATHER STRIPPING
ADJUSTABLE THRESHOLD
GROOVE
TONGUE
SPLIT JAMBS
CASING

**Two basic prehung doors.** The exterior door at far left comes with weather stripping and an adjustable threshold to seal the bottom of the door. Before shipping the door, the distributor bores holes for the locks and installs the exterior casing, called brickmold; you must add separate interior casing (*pages 29-31*) after the door is installed. The horizontal braces keep the lock-side jamb from bowing out of line during installation; the cardboard spacers maintain the correct gap between the door and the jamb.

The interior split-jamb door unit at near left has two jamb sections that fit together with a tongue-and-groove joint. When the section containing the door has been plumbed, shimmed and fastened to the rough frame, the other section is installed from the opposite side of the wall. The casing on both sections is factory-installed; you simply nail it to the rough frame.

# Installing an Exterior Door

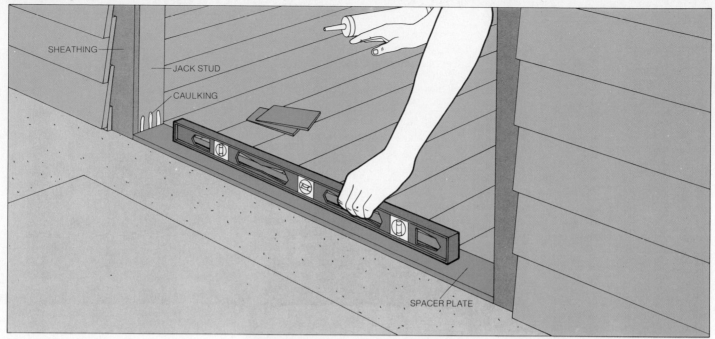

SHEATHING

JACK STUD

CAULKING

SPACER PLATE

**1** **Preparing the opening.** Apply three beads of caulking to the subfloor where the threshold of the new doorframe will rest and continue the beads 6 inches up onto the jack studs at the sides of the opening. If your door unit is not designed to rest on the subfloor, either install the spacer provided by the manufacturer or cut a wooden spacer plate from lumber or exterior-grade plywood as thick as the finish floor—usually ¾ inch; make the plate as wide as the door jambs and long enough to fill the space between the jack studs. Press the spacer into the caulking, with its outside edge flush with the edge of the sheathing, and check it with a carpenter's level. If the spacer is not perfectly horizontal, insert shims below it every 8 inches to level it. Fasten the spacer with galvanized eight-penny common nails in a staggered pattern.

Apply three more beads of caulking on top of the spacer and a long, zigzag bead of caulking to the face of the sheathing around the sides and top of the rough opening. Install a drip cap at the top of the opening (*page 77, Step 3*).

If your door unit is designed to sit on the sub-floor, level the threshold with shims when you set the door in the opening (*Step 2*).

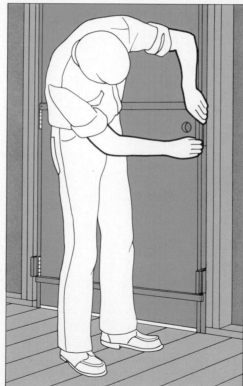

DRIP CAP

BRICKMOLD

**2** **Setting the door in place.** Set the bottom of the unit on the spacer plate and have a helper out-side the house tilt the door upright and hold the brickmold tight against the sheathing. From inside the house, center the unit in the open-ing and, at the heights of the hinges, insert pairs of shims between the side jambs and the jack studs. Do not nail the jambs to the studs yet—the shims will hold the unit temporarily.

**3** **Plumbing the hinge jamb.** Outside the house, hold a level against the face of the hinge-side brickmold; if the brickmold is not per-fectly vertical, pull the jamb out at the top or bottom to plumb it. To hold the brickmold plumb, drive 16-penny finishing nails through the hinge-side jamb and shims at the top and the bottom of the door and into the stud—but do not drive the nails all the way home.

**4** **Squaring the door.** Working inside the house, check the gap between the head jamb and the door. If the gap is wider on the lock side, loosen all of the shims slightly and tighten the pairs of shims at the bottom hinge and the top of the lock-side jamb until the gap is even; if the gap is narrower at the lock side, tighten the shims behind the top hinge and the bottom of the lock-side jamb. Outside the house, make sure the brickmold is still plumb and, at each hinge, drive two 16-penny galvanized finishing nails through the jamb and shims into the jack stud.

Inside the house, remove the braces and spacers installed by the manufacturer and open the door. Remove the two outside screws that fasten the top hinge to the jamb (*inset*) and replace them with the longer ones provided by the manufacturer; the longer screws go through the shims into the jack stud for added support.

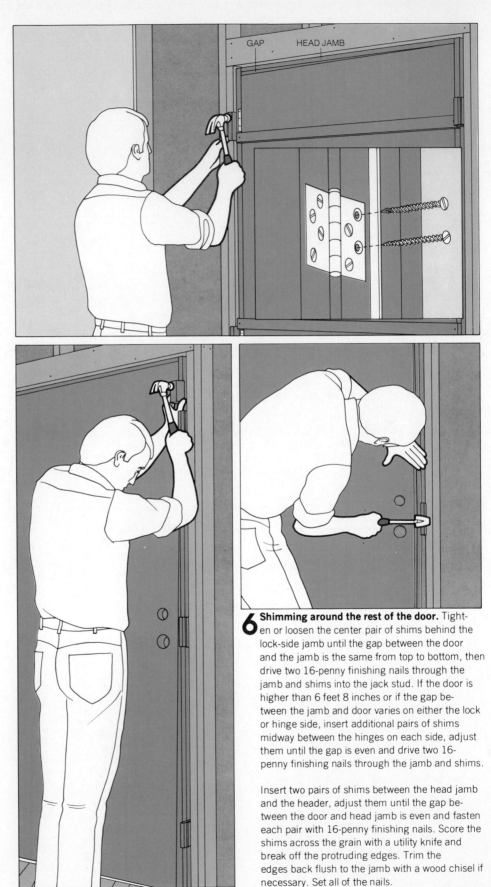

GAP    HEAD JAMB

**5** **Adjusting the lock-side jamb.** Inside the house, check to see whether the top or bottom of the door protrudes beyond the edge of the lock-side jamb; at the same time, have a helper outside check to be sure that the brickmold is tight against the sheathing. If the bottom of the door protrudes inside the house, loosen the shims of the lock-side jamb, hold a block of wood against this jamb near the top and tap the block with a hammer to push the jamb and brickmold outward until the door meets the jamb at both top and bottom. If the top of the door protrudes, push the jamb outward at the bottom.

Have your helper outside the house check to be sure that the door is tight against the stop at both top and bottom; then tighten the pairs of shims at the top and bottom of the lock-side jamb and drive two 16-penny nails partway into the jack stud at each set of shims.

**6** **Shimming around the rest of the door.** Tighten or loosen the center pair of shims behind the lock-side jamb until the gap between the door and the jamb is the same from top to bottom, then drive two 16-penny finishing nails through the jamb and shims into the jack stud. If the door is higher than 6 feet 8 inches or if the gap between the jamb and door varies on either the lock or hinge side, insert additional pairs of shims midway between the hinges on each side, adjust them until the gap is even and drive two 16-penny finishing nails through the jamb and shims.

Insert two pairs of shims between the head jamb and the header, adjust them until the gap between the door and head jamb is even and fasten each pair with 16-penny finishing nails. Score the shims across the grain with a utility knife and break off the protruding edges. Trim the edges back flush to the jamb with a wood chisel if necessary. Set all of the nails.

**7 Adjusting the sill.** Inside the house, close the door and follow the manufacturer's instructions to raise the threshold until a piece of paper slipped beneath the door just catches on the weather stripping. In the widely used model shown here, wedges between the sill and threshold are pushed to the right with the screwdriver, forcing the threshold up; other models have adjusting screws. Do not raise the threshold too high—it can damage the vinyl weather stripping.

Inside the house, fill the space between the jack studs and the side jambs with strips of insulation; outside, caulk the joint between the brickmold and the siding. Install wallboard inside, then install casing to cover the joint between the wallboard and the jambs (*pages 29-31*).

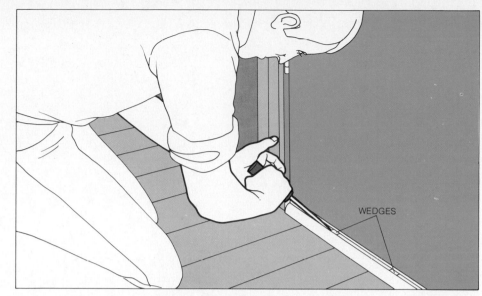

WEDGES

## Aligning a Set of Double Doors

**Squaring the doors.** Center, shim and plumb the doors (*page 99, Steps 1-3*), treating the jamb for the inactive door as you would the hinge-side jamb of a single door. Loosen the pairs of shims behind the top and bottom hinges of both doors and check the gap between each door and the head jamb where the doors meet (*inset*). Tighten the shims behind the top hinge of the higher door until the gap is the same for both doors; then tighten all of the shims, recheck the gap and nail through the jamb of the inactive door with 16-penny galvanized finishing nails. Replace the top-hinge screws of the inactive door with the longer screws provided by the manufacturer (*opposite, Step 4*).

Adjust the active-door jamb as you would the lock-side jamb of a single door, forcing it out at the top or the bottom until the two doors line up perfectly (*opposite, Step 5*). Adjust the gap between the side jambs and the doors as you would for a single door (*opposite, Step 6*).

Insert three sets of shims between the header and the head jamb and adjust them until the gap between the head jamb and the door is even, then drive two 16-penny finishing nails up through each set of shims into the header. Replace the screws on the top hinge of the active door with the longer ones provided by the manufacturer.

# A Split Jamb
# for Interior Walls

**1** **Installing the door.** Slide the jamb section containing the door into the rough opening and insert pairs of shims behind the side jambs at the heights of the hinges; rest the door on two additional shims. Adjust the shims behind the hinge-side jamb until the jamb is plumb. If the gap between the lock-side corner of the head jamb and the door is more than ⅛ inch, remove the door and jamb from the opening and cut back the bottom of the jamb slightly; otherwise have a helper nail the hinge-side casing to the wall.

**2** **Adjusting the casing.** Using a scrap of wood ⅛ inch thick as a gauge, adjust the top casing until there is a ⅛-inch gap between the head jamb and the door, then nail the casing to the header. Adjust the gap between the door and the lock-side jamb similarly and nail the lock-side casing. From the other side of the door, insert pairs of shims above the head jamb, behind the middle of the hinge-side jamb and behind the lock-side jamb. Drive two 16-penny finishing nails through each pair and cut the shims off.

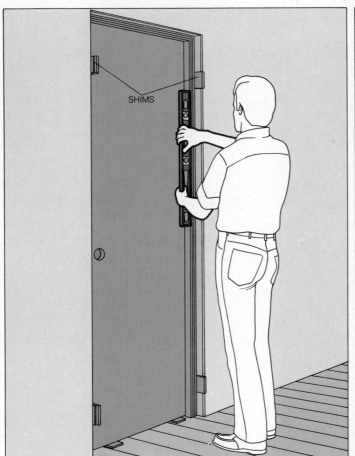

SHIMS

⅛" GAUGE

**3** **Installing the other half of the jamb.** Fit the tongue of the back jamb into the groove of the door jamb (*inset*) and push the back jamb inward until its casing rests against the wallboard. Fasten the casing with eightpenny finishing nails, then drive 16-penny finishing nails through the jambs into the rough framing.

# Choosing and Fitting the Lock

You need only one tool to put in an ordinary lock—a screwdriver. The lock manufacturer provides the hardware and, if you buy the lock before you order a prehung door and give the template and specifications that come with the lock to the door supplier, he will bore the necessary holes in the door and jamb.

Door locks and latches come in four main types. A passage latch for an interior door has knobs and bolt, but no locking mechanism; a privacy lock *(right),* for bedrooms and bathrooms, can be locked from the inside with a push button.

An entrance lock *(below, left)* can be locked from both sides—with a key from outside, a push button inside. The type with a dead-locking plunger, which locks the bolt when the door is shut, is more difficult to pick. For extra security add a dead-bolt lock *(below, right),* which has a heavy bolt that slides into the jamb.

**A privacy lock.** Screw the strike plate to the jamb; slip the latch bolt into its hole in the door, with the beveled side of the bolt facing the strike plate as the door is closed, and screw the latch-bolt plate to the door. Depress the latch bolt about ⅛ inch and slip the outside-knob unit

into the door, sliding the screw posts, spindle tongue and (for privacy locksets) the locking bar through the latch-bolt holes. Slide the inside-knob unit onto the spindle tongue and locking bar, align its holes with the screw posts and fasten the knob units together with machine screws.

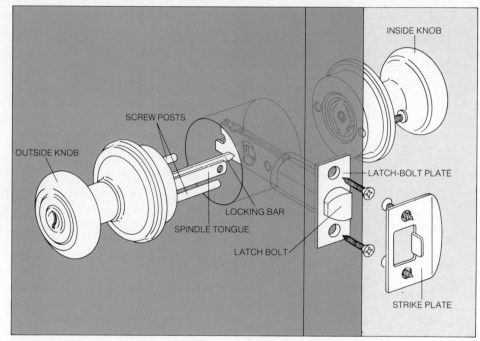

**An entrance lock.** Install strike plate and latch bolt as you would on a privacy lock *(above).* Remove the interior-knob assembly according to the manufacturer's instructions: For this widely used model, depress the knob catch with the tip of a screwdriver, then slide the interior knob, interior rose and mounting plate off the spindle. Adjust the lock for the thickness of the door by turning the threaded exterior rose. Depress the latch bolt slightly and slip the spindle into

place from the outside until the cylinder engages the prongs of the latch bolt.

Replace the interior-knob assembly; in this model this is done in three steps: First fasten the mounting plate to the cylinder with machine screws; then slide the interior rose over the spindle and snap it onto the spring clip in the plate; finally, slide the knob onto the spindle until its slot fits over the knob catch.

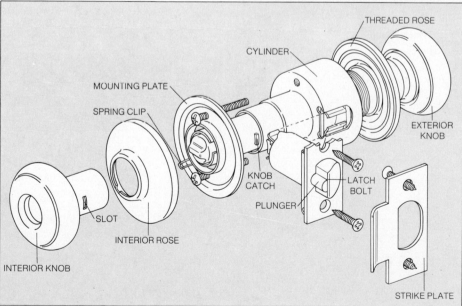

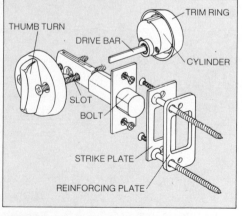

**A dead-bolt lock.** Fasten the steel reinforcing plate through the jamb into the stud with 3-inch screws, then fasten the brass strike plate over the steel one. Turn the tip of a screwdriver in the slot of the bolt assembly to extend the bolt, slip the assembly into the door with the drive-bar slot down and screw the bolt plate to the door. Adjust the lock for the thickness of the door: on this model, you can select a trim ring of the correct thickness; on others, you may have to cut off the tip of the drive bar.

Slide the cylinder into the door from outside, slipping the drive bar through the bolt-assembly slot and aligning the cylinder and assembly holes. Slide the thumb turn into position over the drive bar and screw it to the cylinder.

# The Space Savers: Sliding Doors for Tight Places

Sliding glass doors, running on rollers along a track, combine the transparency of a huge window with the convenience of a door; as an opening between house and yard, they unite two spaces visually and physically. The pocket door *(page 107)*, a variation of the sliding door, glides into a metal frame that is built into the wall and then covered with wallboard. Both are practical solutions to the problem of a space that has no room for a conventional hinged door to swing.

Sliding doors are sold in kits containing finished door panels, a frame and all the needed hardware. Door frames, of wood or aluminum, come in widths from 5 to 20 feet and in heights from 6½ to 8 feet. Wooden doors are more expensive than the metal models, but are more efficient insulators. If you live in a climate of extreme temperatures but prefer a metal door, you can get a type in which the hollow parts of the metal framing are filled with insulation. The widely used type of wooden sliding door shown on these pages has two door panels, one stationary and one movable, but three- and four-panel units are also available.

Whatever kit you buy, check its contents carefully. Many building codes require the almost-shatterproof tempered glass. In addition, check to be sure that the flexible weather stripping, which seals the unit along the line where the panels meet, fits tightly.

Start the installation with a rough opening *(Chapter 2)* ⅜ inch higher at the top and wider at each side than the doorframe; for a sliding door take special pains to make the opening plumb and square because the clearances are critical. Run three parallel beads of caulking along the subfloor and set the frame into the opening from the outside. Press the frame down to distribute the caulking.

Both wooden and metal doors are screwed into the rough framing at the jamb, but the details of the trim differ slightly for the two materials: kits for wooden doors come with special wooden casings that are nailed to the outside of the house to help secure the frame; metal frames are trimmed outside the house with ordinary wooden brickmold. Inside the house, both wooden and metal frames are finished with conventional interior wooden trim.

**1 Securing the threshold.** After assembling the frame and caulking the subfloor along the sill, have a helper hold the frame against the sides of the opening as you nail the interior edge of the threshold to the sill every 12 inches.

**2** **Fastening the frame.** While the helper checks with a level, plumb the frame (*right*) by hammering shims—five pairs between each side jamb and jack stud and three pairs between the head jamb and the header. Secure the frame temporarily with nails, a foot apart, driven halfway through the brickmold into the rough frame.

Screw the jambs to the jack studs and the header through the predrilled holes. Then drive the nails the rest of the way in and install metal flashing as a drip cap (*page 77, Step 3*) over the head brickmold.

**3** **Supporting the threshold.** Cut a piece of scrap wood to the width and thickness of the threshold overhang, align it under the threshold and against the exterior sheathing and nail it to the sheathing (*above*).

**4** **Installing the stationary panel.** Lift the panel into the outside channel of the frame and slide it into the side jamb. If the panel does not slide all the way into the jamb, force it in by pushing down on a length of 2-by-4 angled between the panel and the opposite side jamb. Screw the bottom and top angle brackets provided by the manufacturer to the threshold and the head jamb.

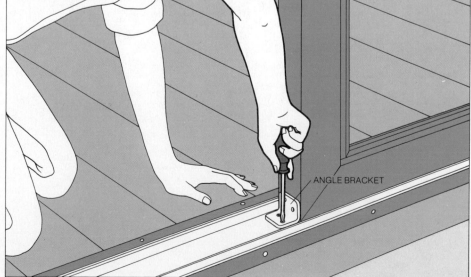

ANGLE BRACKET

**5** **Fastening the parting strip.** Screw the parting strip, which separates the stationary and movable panels, into the stationary panel. In the typical model shown here, the strip is located in a rabbet along the center of the jamb.

**6** **Installing the movable panel.** Most movable wooden panels are put in by setting the rollers into the inside channel of the frame and tilting the door into the channel at the top of the frame (*below*). Then set the head stop into the shallow rabbet along the underside of the head jamb and screw the stop to the jamb. Fit the stop snugly against the weather stripping.

In some models the head stop is an integral part of the frame. With this type, angle the top of the movable panel into place behind the stop, swing the bottom inward and ease the panel down until the rollers rest in the channel.

PARTING STRIP

ROLLER ADJUSTMENT SCREW

**7** **Plumbing the movable panel.** Close the movable panel. If it is not plumb against the side jamb, pry off the plastic guard caps in the bottom rail and turn the height-adjustment screws (*above*), which raise or lower the door over the rollers, until the door meets the side jamb squarely.

# A Door that Slides into the Wall

A traditional type of sliding door, the pocket door, can be put to good use in a modern house where rooms are compact and wall space is precious. A passageway between a kitchen and dining room, for example, often has little room on either side for a conventional door to swing open—but a pocket door seems to disappear as it opens. It takes up no usable wall space, for it slides inside the wall, filling a channel, or pocket, formed by a prefabricated finish frame.

The frame generally includes a steel split jamb and split stud through which the door slides, wooden nailing strips, an overhead track and such hardware as brackets, gliders, machine screws and special nails. Most frames accommodate doors up to 6 feet 8 inches high and from ¾ to 1¾ inches thick. The best models, like the one shown on these pages, have tracks that telescope to accept doors from 2 to 3 feet wide; other models have fixed tracks, which can be cut down for a door less than 3 feet wide. The door itself, preferably a hollow-core interior door, must be bought separately, along with the door hardware—a pull and, if you like, a lock. To complete the frame, you will need standard stop, jamb and casing stock; to enclose the pocket, use wallboard or other covering to match the rest of the wall.

## Installing a Pocket Door

**1** **Cutting the nailing strips.** If your unit has a telescoping overhead track, unscrew the wooden nailing strips from the sides of the track. Using a backsaw and miter box, cut the strips 1¼ inches longer than the width of the door; the cuts must be perfectly square. Replace the nailing strips and loosen the two screws that secure the center bracket of the track. Telescope the track to the width of the opening and tighten the center-bracket screws.

If your model has a fixed overhead track, cut the nailing strips with a handsaw to the length specified by the manufacturer, then cut through the track with a hacksaw and affix the end brackets provided by the manufacturer.

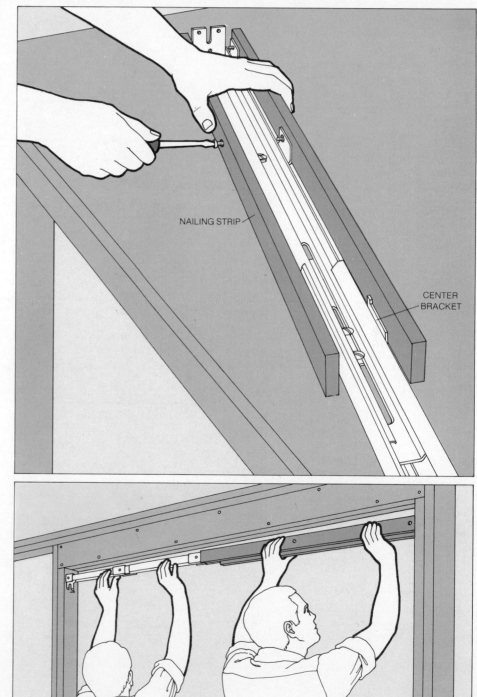

NAILING STRIP

CENTER BRACKET

**2** **Hanging the overhead track.** Drive nails partway into the centers of the jack studs 1½ inches higher than the door and with a helper hang the track on the nails. Have a helper raise the lower end until the track is horizontal, then nail both ends of the track to the jack studs.

Snap chalk lines on the floor between the bottom edges of the jack studs so that you can locate the bottom positions of the split jamb and split stud later (*page 108, Step 4*).

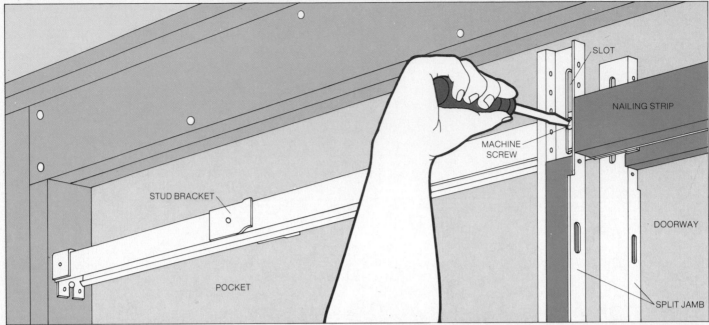

SLOT

NAILING STRIP

MACHINE SCREW

STUD BRACKET

DOORWAY

POCKET

SPLIT JAMB

**3** **Fastening jamb and stud to the track.** Rest the split jamb on the floor, and fit its top over the center bracket of the track and against the ends of the nailing strips. Drive the machine screws provided by the manufacturer through the slots of the jamb top into the holes in the bracket. On a telescoping track, tighten the two screws at the bottom of the bracket as well.

Mount the split stud in the same way: fasten it in the fixed stud bracket located over the center of the pocket and nail it to the floor.

**4** **Fastening jamb and stud to the floor.** Set the nailing plate at the bottom of the split jamb between the chalk lines marked in Step 2, plumb the jamb with a carpenter's level and nail the plate to the floor. Repeat the procedure with the split stud. At the top of the jamb, nail through the jamb flanges into the edges of the nailing strips for each track (inset).

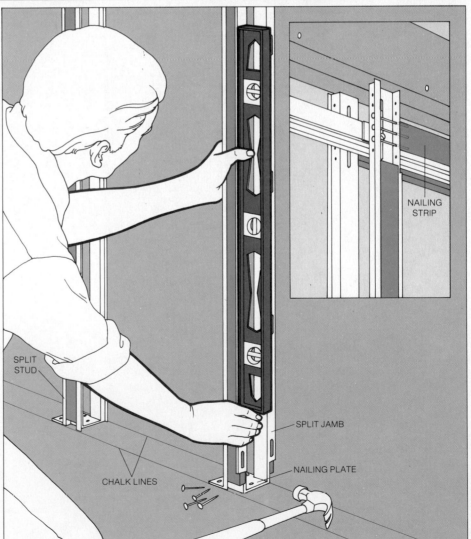

NAILING STRIP

SPLIT STUD

SPLIT JAMB

NAILING PLATE

CHALK LINES

**5** **Hanging the door.** Draw a center line along the top edge of the door and, following the manufacturer's spacing instructions, drive the four screws provided by the manufacturer until the screw heads are within ¼ inch of the surface (*inset*). Loosen the adjusting screw on one of the gliders, extend the slotted bracket and fit the glider wheel into the part of the track that runs into the door pocket; then, holding the door partway inside the pocket with a helper, push the slots of the glider bracket under one pair of screws and tighten the screws. Slide the door farther into the pocket and install the second glider in the same way, setting its wheel in the part of the track that runs across the doorway. On the telescoping track shown here, the two gliders should face in opposite directions.

Plumb the door and adjust its height above the floor by moving the glider brackets along their slots, then tighten the adjusting screws.

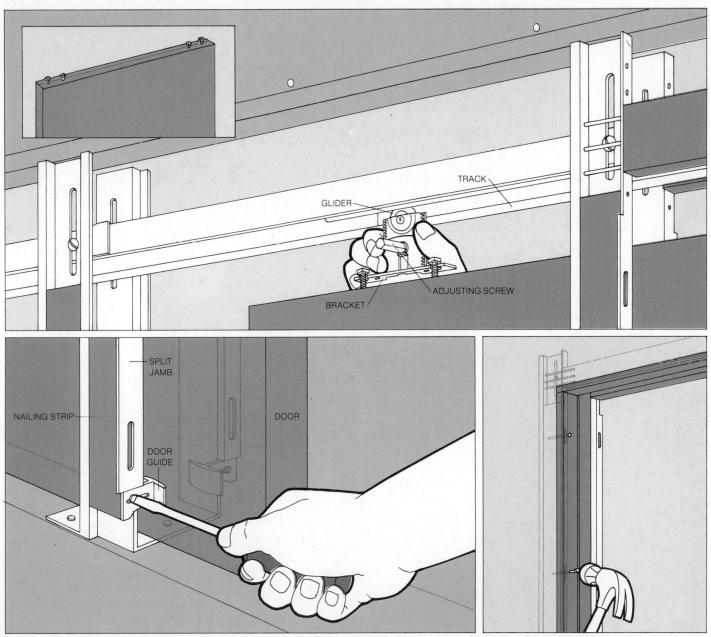

TRACK

GLIDER

ADJUSTING SCREW

BRACKET

SPLIT JAMB

NAILING STRIP

DOOR

DOOR GUIDE

DOOR

**6** **Hardware to hold the door in line.** Set the slotted section of each door guide against the edge of the wooden nailing strip at the bottom of the split jamb, and drive the screw provided by the manufacturer through the slot and partially into the strip. Locate each guide ⅛ inch from the door and tighten the screw.

Using the screw provided by the manufacturer, fasten the rubber bumper to the pocket jack stud, 41 inches above the floor. Slide the door against the bumper. The outer edge of the door should extend ⅜ inch into the doorway; if it does not, either shim the bumper with a metal washer or trim it with a utility knife.

Install wallboard above the opening and over the pocket, using the rough frame, the track nailing strips and the wooden strips on the split jamb and split stud as nailing surfaces.

**7** **Installing stop, jamb and casing.** Nail standard doorstop stock to the bottom of the track nailing strips, covering the edges of the wallboard above and extending to within ⅛ inch of the door. Nail stop stock to the split jamb on both sides of the pocket opening; nail through the slots of the split jamb into the jamb nailing strips. At the other side of the rough frame, fasten jamb stock to the jack stud. Install casing (*pages 29-31*) overhead and at the sides of the doorway.

# A Modern Garage Door that Comes in a Kit

Despite its size and elaborate hardware, a new garage door is surprisingly easy to install—the job consists mainly of assembling prefitted pieces from a kit. It should take no more than a day, once the rough frame has been prepared (Chapter 2).

Sectional overhead doors like the one shown on these pages offer several advantages over the old-fashioned hinged doors and the one-piece swing-up doors (called shin busters in the trade, because they also swing out). A sectional door requires no clearance outside the garage; it opens and closes easily even when deep snow covers the driveway. The powerful springs that balance the door are high overhead, clear of clothing and fingers, and the spring tension matches the opening and closing cycle, so that the door works smoothly, with little effort. In addition, a sectional door is the best type of door for use with an electrically powered door opener.

Sectional doors are manufactured in several standard sizes. For about twice the price of a standard door, you can order one custom-cut for an odd-sized opening, but it is usually faster and less expensive to alter the opening to one of the standard door sizes. Your garage must have enough space to accommodate the overhead tracks and springs, which generally extend back from the opening approximately 15 inches more than the height of the door.

A two-car door is generally fitted with torsion springs—coils that rotate a shaft running across the top of the opening. A one-car door is more likely to be fitted with extension springs that stretch along the overhead tracks.

Either type of spring can cause the metal parts to flail violently if accidentally released, and extreme caution is required during installation. Torsion springs are tightened and adjusted with steel winding rods that fit into holes in the spring assembly. Be sure that the rods fit the holes exactly, and keep your head and body clear of the path of the rods as you wind. Extension springs should be installed and adjusted with the door propped open, so that the springs and cables are not under tension.

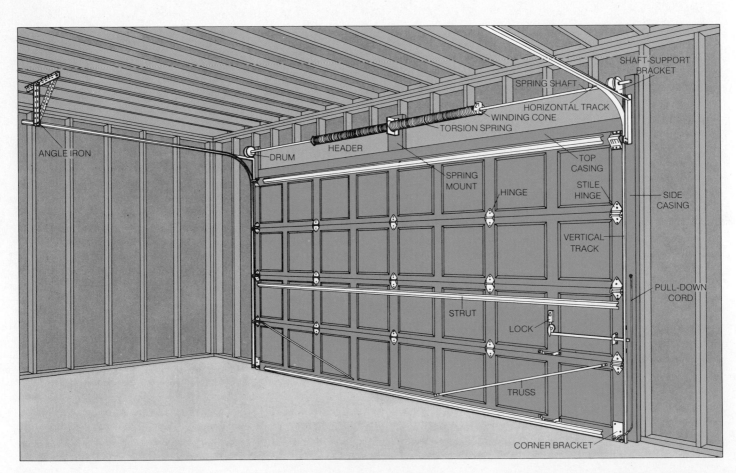

**Anatomy of a sectional door.** Horizontal sections hinged together make up this typical overhead door. The hinges along each side of the door and the brackets at the corners contain rollers. The rollers ride in tracks set on 2-by-4 side casings around the door opening; the tracks extend horizontally into the garage and are secured to the ceiling joists with angle irons. A reinforcing strut and two diagonal metal trusses add rigidity to the bottom of the door. In this example the door is fitted with torsion springs (for the details of an extension-spring assembly, see page 115). Cables run from the bottom corner brackets of the door to drums on a spring shaft mounted over the door opening. The shaft is turned with the help of two torsion springs, which are adjusted by winding cones to counterbalance the door's weight.

# Installing the Sections

**1 Trimming the opening.** Before you install the door itself, line the opening with a casing and stops (*inset*). For the side casings, cut 2-by-4s about a foot longer than the opening height and screw them to the jack studs and header, flush with the inner edges of the side jambs. As a top casing, screw a third 2-by-4 between the side casings, attaching it to the header directly above the top of the opening. For an opening more than 8 feet wide, supplement the top casing with a spring mount—use a 1-foot length of 2-by-6 and nail it vertically to the header and to a cripple stud or a block directly above the center of the top casing.

Temporarily nail wooden stops to the sides and top of the door opening, placing their edges flush with the inner edges of the casing.

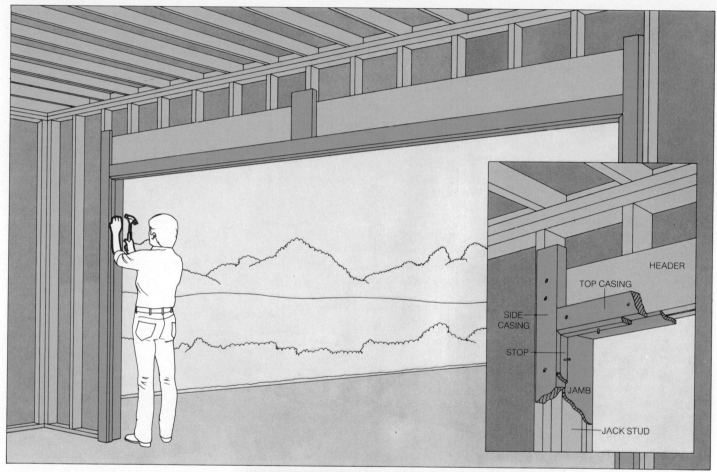

**2 Leveling the bottom section.** Set the bottom section of the door in place against the stops inside the opening, check it with a carpenter's level and have a helper drive a shim under the low end until the section is level.

Open a compass to the widest distance between the floor and the bottom of the leveled section. Then set the point of the compass on the floor and the pencil end against the bottom rail of the section and, holding the compass point tight against the floor, draw a horizontal line along the rail (*inset*). At each end of the section, note the distance between the line and the bottom edge of the section, and mark the distance on the bottom end of the corresponding vertical track. Trim section and tracks at the marks.

**3** **Mounting the hardware.** Using the hardware supplied by the manufacturer (a typical connection assembly is shown at right), attach the cables to the corner brackets of the bottom section with clevis pins, notching the section if necessary. Bolt the brackets into the predrilled holes in the bottom corners of the section. Along the bottom edge, nail the rubber weatherproofing gasket, using roofing nails spaced 2 feet apart.

Bolt the bottom leaves of the hinges into place on the top rails of all but the top section, and bolt the top corner brackets to the top section. Screw on the door handles (typically, to the bottom rails of the bottom and second sections) and attach the lock. Attach the reinforcing struts to the bottom rail of the bottom section, the top rail of the top section and to a section near the center; if your door comes with trusses to add rigidity to the bottom section, attach them.

**4** **Stacking the sections.** With a helper, center the first section across the opening, then drive two nails partway into the casing next to each end of the section and hammer the nailheads around the edge of the section to hold it in place. Secure the other sections above the first in the same way, attach the upper leaves of the hinges and install the rollers in the outside hinges and corner brackets. Tie a pull-down cord to the bottom roller shaft nearest the handle and to an eye hook screwed to the adjoining side casing just above the midpoint of the door.

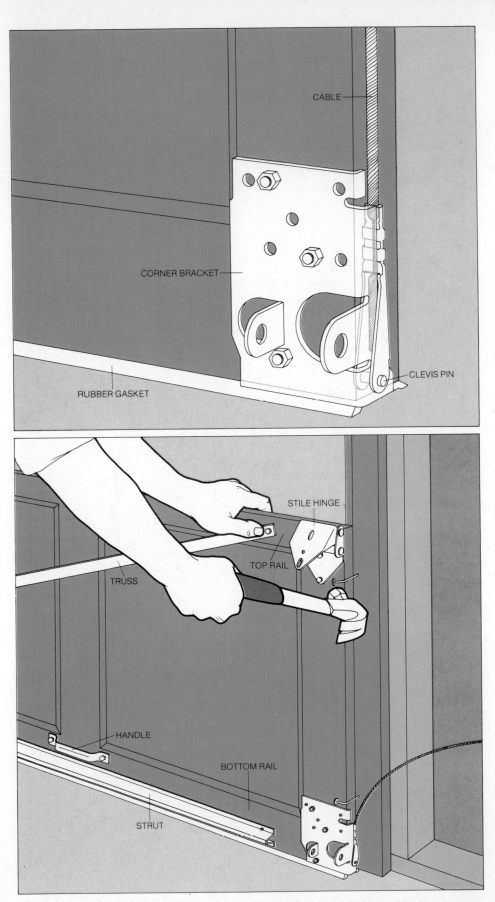

CABLE

CORNER BRACKET

CLEVIS PIN

RUBBER GASKET

STILE HINGE

TOP RAIL

TRUSS

HANDLE

BOTTOM RAIL

STRUT

**5** **Putting up the tracks.** Bolt the horizontal and vertical tracks together on the ground and attach their mounting brackets or supports for springs *(inset)*; then, with a helper, fit each vertical track over the door rollers and lag-bolt the tracks to the casing, leaving ½ inch between the edges of the door and the tracks. Tie the horizontal tracks temporarily to ceiling joists.

Install the door-locking mechanism, and then lock the door in preparation for mounting the torsion spring and cables.

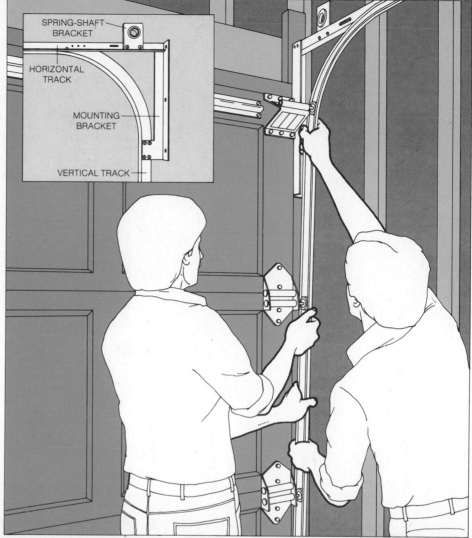

**6** **Mounting the torsion-spring assembly.** Mount the torsion-spring assembly on the spring shaft according to the manufacturer's instructions (the inset shows a typical arrangement) and, with a helper, insert the ends of the shaft into the spring-shaft brackets on the horizontal tracks. For a wide door, lag-bolt the support bracket at the center of the shaft to the 2-by-6 spring mount over the top casing; for a one-car door, mount the spring at the side specified by the manufacturer.

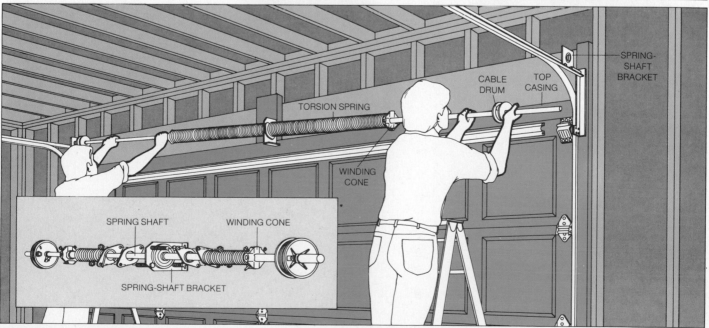

**7 Winding the springs.** Insert the winding rods into adjoining holes on a winding cone and tighten the springs by pushing the rods upward, moving them from hole to hole as you turn the cone. To count the turns, draw a horizontal chalk line across the coils of the springs before you begin winding: each complete spiral of the line equals a complete turn. Caution: wind the springs slowly and carefully, keeping your body clear of the path of the rods and maintaining a firm grip on the ends of the rods.

When you have wound a spring, leave one rod in the winding cone, braced against the strut at the top of the door *(inset)*; tighten the cone's setscrews but leave the rod in place.

**8 Connecting cables.** At each side of the door, thread a cable up between the roller shafts and the 2-by-4 side casing, wrap the cable around its drum according to the manufacturer's instructions and fasten it to the drum—in most models, with a cap screw. Position the drum, tighten its setscrews and remove the cone's bracing rod, following the manufacturer's instructions.

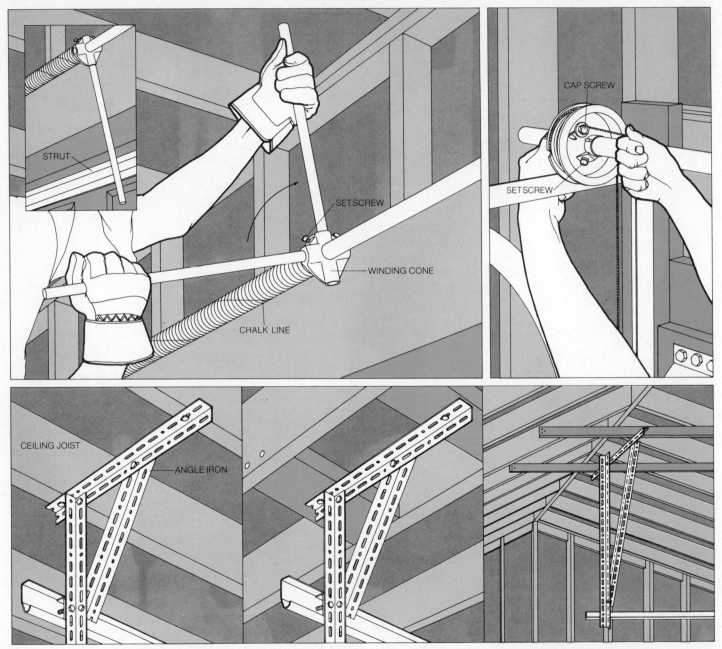

STRUT

SET SCREW

WINDING CONE

CHALK LINE

CAP SCREW

SETSCREW

CEILING JOIST

ANGLE IRON

**9 Supporting the horizontal track.** If the ceiling joists are parallel to the horizontal tracks *(left)*, lag-bolt a slotted angle iron (available from building-supply dealers) across the joists, just above the mounting hole of each track. Raise the free end of each track to a level 1 inch higher than the door end of the track, then cut a piece of angle iron to fit vertically between the mounting hole and the horizontal angle iron and bolt it in place. Have a helper raise the door until two sections are within the horizontal tracks and move the tracks sideways to set a ½-inch gap between each track and the edges of the door, then cut and bolt a brace between the vertical and horizontal angle irons. If the ceiling joists are perpendicular to the horizontal tracks *(center)*, nail 2-by-4 blocks between the joists that flank the track mounting holes and fasten the horizontal angle iron to the blocks. If there are no ceiling joists, put up a collar beam to hold the track ends *(right)*. Close the door from the outside and check the stop positions—they should be ⅛ inch from the door. Move them if necessary and nail them in place.

# Extension Springs for a Narrow Door

**1** **Mounting the pulleys and springs.** Assemble the sections and tracks *(pages 110-113, Steps 1-6)*, then prop the door partway open with 2-by-4s and fasten the horizontal tracks to the ceiling joists *(opposite, Step 9)*. Open the door completely and prop it in place. Hook the ends of the extension springs through holes in the vertical angle irons about 12 inches above the tracks. Attach spring pulleys to the other ends of the springs, using clevis pins, bolts, lock washers and nuts. Then bolt stud pulleys to the track-mounting brackets on the casing.

**2** **Threading the cables.** Run the cables from the bottom corner brackets over the tops of the stud and the spring pulleys and back toward the door. Anchor the cables to the track-mounting brackets according to the instructions—typically, by threading them through holes in the track-mounting brackets—cut off the excess cable, and equalize the slack of the cables.

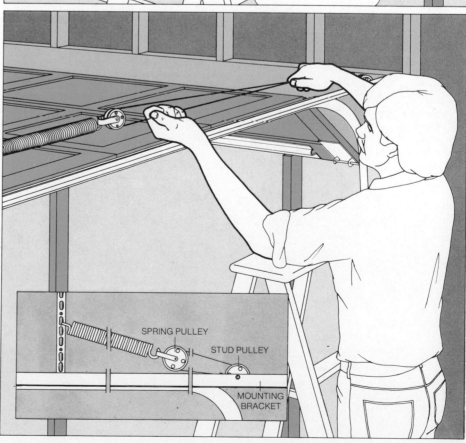

SPRING PULLEY

STUD PULLEY

MOUNTING BRACKET

# The Fine Art of Fitting and Hanging a Door

A prehung door complete with its jambs (pages 98-102) provides an easy way to fill a door opening—but not necessarily the best or only way. Sometimes you must hang a door in existing jambs because the door—and only the door—needs replacing. At other times you must build new jambs, because the space available for an opening does not match any prehung door or because the door you have chosen—a swinging door, perhaps—does not come prehung. Both jobs call for special preparations and some specialized carpentry techniques.

Of the two jobs, the first is by far the easier. You must be sure, of course, that the new door will fit the old opening in height, width and thickness. You should be able to find one of matching thickness, but you may have to settle for one that is slightly oversize in height and width, and then trim it to fit. You can take as much as an inch off the height of a panel or hollow-core door, and as much as 2 inches off the width; trim the width equally from both sides, but trim

the height from the bottom alone. If you must cut off more than an inch from the bottom, order a plain, solid-core door—called a flush door—which can be cut back any reasonable amount on any side.

To build a finish frame for a new opening (pages 116-119), order jamb stock an inch thick for an exterior door, ¾ inch for an interior door. The width depends on how your walls are made. Use stock 4⅝ inches wide for standard 2-by-4 stud walls covered with wallboard and 5⅜ inches wide for walls that are covered with plaster. For walls of different thicknesses, have the lumberyard mill pieces of jamb stock to the width you need or trim the stock yourself with a plane.

Two grades of jamb stock are generally available. The more costly "clear" stock, made from selected lumber, can be finished with stain or varnish, which will reveal the grain of the wood; finger-joint stock, consisting of a number of short pieces of wood glued together, must be covered with paint.

Assembling the jambs involves joint

techniques like those required for windows. Grooves called dadoes seat the head jamb between the side jambs, and the hinges fit into recessed insets, called mortises, in the side jambs and the door. Professionals often use a router for these cuts, but a backsaw and a sharp chisel are just as effective. For accuracy in measurement, use a combination square and a marking gauge (Steps 2-5).

Order such accessories as hinges, locks and thresholds when you buy the door and the jamb stock. A solid-core door or any door taller than 6 feet 8 inches requires three hinges. Buy rectangular hinges, which are easier to install than the round-cornered ones used on most prehung doors. For both exterior and interior doors, buy locks that adjust to fit the door thickness. If you plan to install a dead-bolt lock in addition to the knob lock, be sure that the backset—the distance between the center of each lock and the edge of the door—is the same for both so that the locks line up vertically on the face of the door.

## Making the Side Jambs

**1** **Locating dadoes in the jambs.** On two pieces of jamb stock, mark the height of the door plus clearance for a rug or threshold, add a second mark above the first at a distance equal to the thickness of the stock, and extend both marks across the width of the stock with a combination square. Cut the jambs 1 inch above the dadoes.

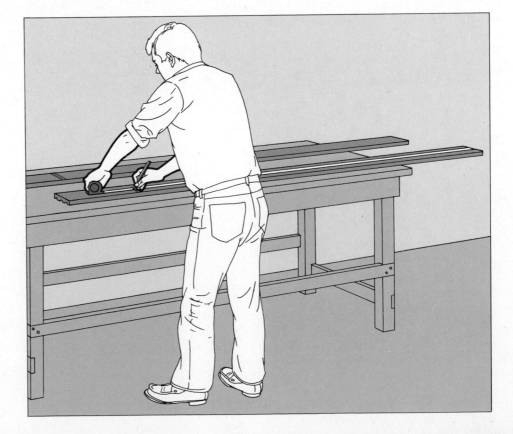

**2 Cutting the dadoes.** Clamp each of the pieces to the top of a workbench and, with a marking gauge set to half the thickness of the stock, mark the gain—that is, the depth of the dado—on both edges of the jamb stock. Cut out the dado grooves with a saw and a chisel, as shown on pages 89-90, Steps 2 through 4.

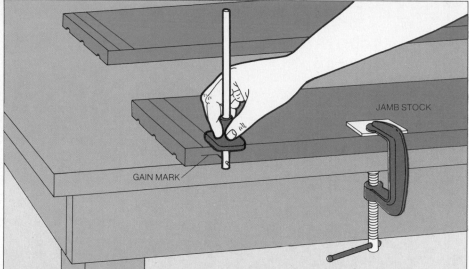

JAMB STOCK

GAIN MARK

**3 Locating the hinges.** On one of the side jambs make one mark 7 inches below the bottom of the dado and another 11 inches above the bottom of the jamb; extend both marks across the width of the jamb and set a hinge, pin side out, against each marked line. Score along the top and bottom of each hinge with a utility knife. If the door requires a third hinge, center it between the marks for the top and bottom hinges and score its location in the same way.

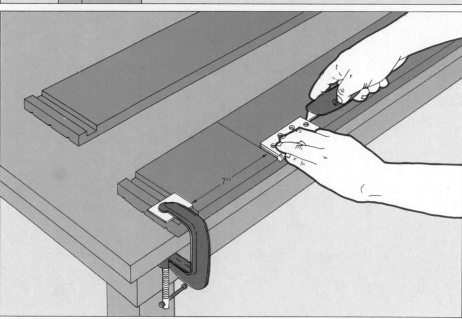

7"

**4 Marking the depth of the mortises.** Set the marking gauge to the thickness of a hinge leaf (you need not measure the thickness; simply set the needle of the gauge at one side of the leaf and the plate of the gauge at the other). Run the gauge along the edge of the jamb between the lines scored for each hinge.

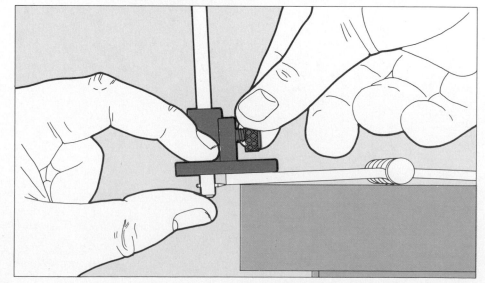

**5** **Completing the mortise marks.** Set the marking gauge to the thickness of the door less $3/16$ inch and connect the scored hinge lines on the face of the jamb. Using a utility knife and a straightedge, deeply score all the hinge lines on the face and edge of the jamb.

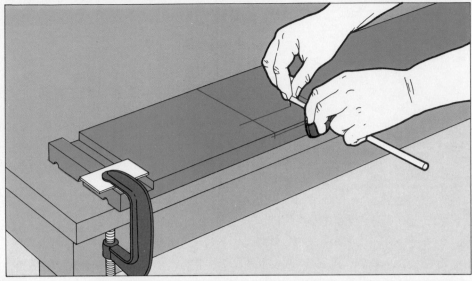

**6** **Chiseling out the mortises.** Use a mallet to drive a $1\frac{1}{4}$-inch wood chisel, held vertically with beveled edge inward, along the scored mortise marks on the face of the jamb (below, left). Then make a series of cuts inside the mortise areas, at a right angle to the edge of the jamb (below, center), tilting the chisel slightly. Next, chisel from the opposite direction to cut out the chiseled wedges. Finally, place the flat edge of the chisel against each gain mark and clean out the whole mortise (below, right).

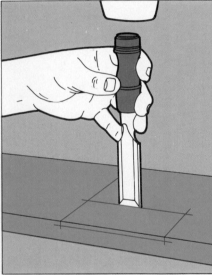

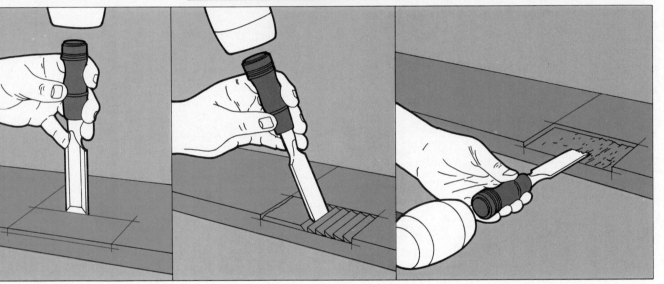

## Assembling the Finish Frame

**1** **Assembling the frame.** Place a side jamb in a vise, sandwiched between strips of cardboard to protect it from damage, and, on the outside of the jamb, use a combination square to draw a line corresponding to the center of the dado. Insert a head jamb, cut to the width of the door plus the total depth of the dadoes, into the dado. Countersink and drive two $1\frac{1}{2}$-inch screws along the line into the head jamb. Fasten the other side jamb to the head jamb in the same way. Using the technique on page 121, Step 5, plane a slight bevel on the outer edge of the jamb so that the casing will fit snugly against the wall.

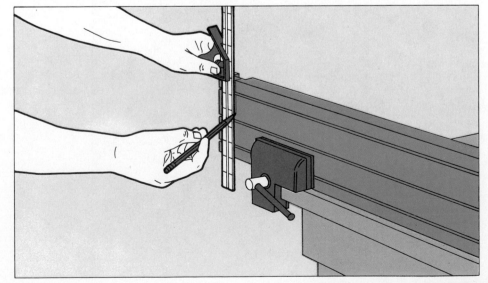

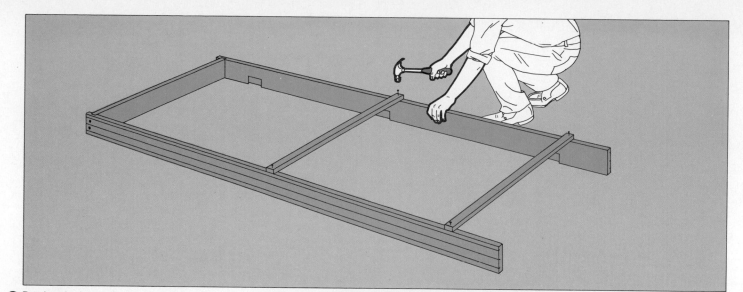

**2** **Bracing the frame.** Cut two 1-by-2 spreaders to a length equal to the outer width of the assembled frame. Tack the spreaders to the edges of the side jambs so that they span the finish-frame opening at locations just below the center and bottom hinge mortises.

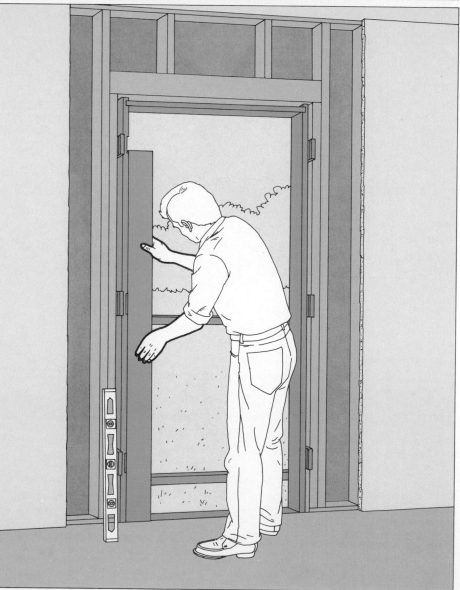

**3** **Fitting the frame in place.** Center the frame in the rough opening, push shims between the side jambs and the jack studs, and use a level and a 6-foot length of ¾-inch plywood to be sure that the side jambs are plumb and straight, adjusting the shims to eliminate warps or bows. Fasten the side jambs to the jack studs (*pages 99-100, Steps 1-6*).

## Fitting the Door to the Frame

**1 Marking the height.** Measure the distance from the floor to the bottom of the head jamb and subtract ½ inch plus clearance for a rug or threshold; measure and mark this distance down from the top of the door. Extend the mark across the width of the bottom of the door, using a combination square or a marking gauge. If the door has a plywood-veneer face, score the line deeply with a utility knife and score a matching line on the other side of the door.

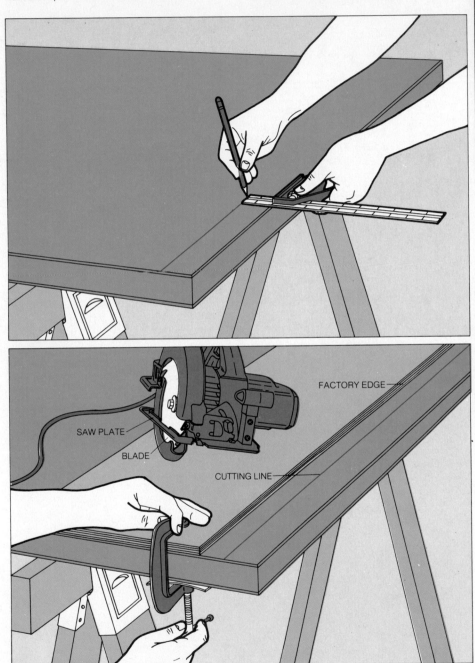

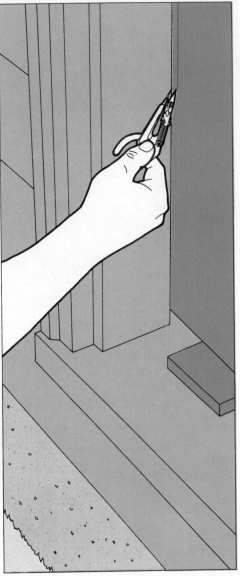

**2 Cutting the door down.** Above the cutting line *(Step 1)*, draw a mark across the door at the distance between the blade of a circular saw and the edge of the saw plate; clamp the straight, factory-cut edge of a piece of plywood on this line. Saw along the plywood guide, with the blade set ⅛ inch deeper than the door thickness.

**3 Sizing for width.** Set the hinge-side edge of the door against the side jamb and wedge the top against the head jamb. With a helper holding the door from the other side, scribe the lock-side face of the door by running a compass set to ⅛ inch along the jamb. Plane the door down to the line.

If the clearance at the head jamb is not even, set the points of the compass at the widest point of the gap, scribe the top of the door and plane the top down to the scribed line.

Tack stops *(page 32, Steps 1 and 2)* to the head and side jambs, positioning them so as to allow for the thickness of the door plus a clearance of ¹⁄₁₆ inch.

**4** **Marking the bevel.** Set the spur of a marking gauge to exactly ⅛ inch. On the face of the door that will meet the doorstop, run the marking gauge along the lock-side edge. Using a ruler, draw lines across the top and bottom edges of the door to the adjacent corners.

**5** **Planing the bevel.** Set the door on a door jack, adjust a jack plane (*page 22*) for a slanting cut on the edge of the door and plane down to the line made by the marking gauge (*inset*); then straighten the plane iron and trim away the hump along the middle of the edge.

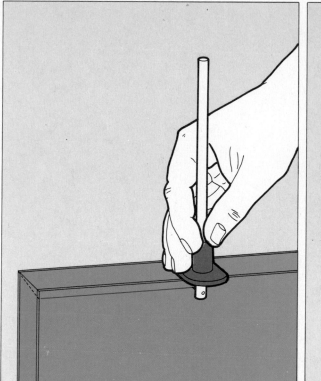

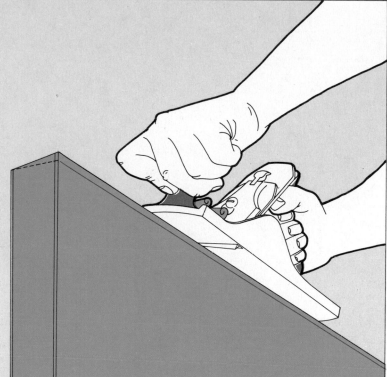

## A Door Jack for Easier Work

A simple device called a door jack, which can be assembled from a few scraps of wood and cardboard, offers a handy way to hold a door in place while planing it to size or cutting hinge mortises. It is fashioned from small scraps of lumber: three 1-by-2s and two 2-by-6s.

The 2-by-6s, separated by a gap ⅜ inch wider than the thickness of the door, are nailed on edge to a 1-by-2. Cardboard strips lining this gap protect the door finish during the work; a pair of 1-by-2s, nailed across the bottom of the assembly and tacked to the floor, stabilize the jack and raise it above the floor. When the door is set into the jack, its weight forces the middle of the flexible 1-by-2 down toward the floor, and the 2-by-6s squeeze together to seize the sides of the door and hold the top steady.

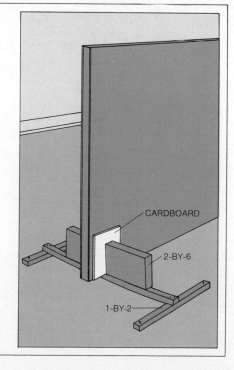

CARDBOARD

2-BY-6

1-BY-2

## Putting on the Hinges

**1** **Determining the hinge locations.** With the door in the finish frame, have a helper hold two fourpenny nails as spacers between the top of the door and the head jamb while you drive shims beneath the door to wedge it tight against the nails. Drive a shim between the door and the lock-side jamb about 3 feet from the floor, to push the door against the hinge-side jamb; then nick the edge of the door with a utility knife at the top and bottom of each hinge mortise in the jamb.

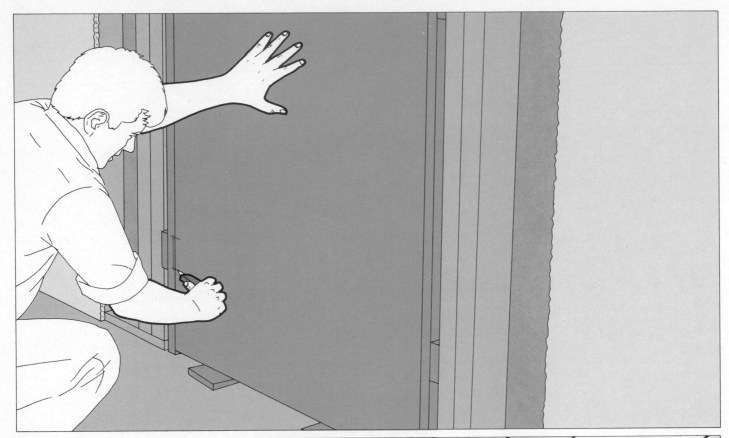

**2** **Mortising the hinge.** Take the door out of the frame and extend the marks across the hinge-side edge. Run a marking gauge, set to $^3/_{16}$ inch less than the thickness of the door, between each pair of hinge marks to outline the mortise to be cut; hold the gauge so that the $^3/_{16}$-inch strip to be left uncut is on the side abutting the doorstop. Chisel out the hinge mortises in the door (*page 118, Step 6*). Separate the hinge leaves and screw them to the door and the jamb, making sure they are right side up.

Set the door upright beside the hinge-side jamb and slip a pair of shims between the floor and the lock-side corner of the door. Slip the top hinge together and insert the hinge pin; then slip the leaves of the lower hinges together. If the hinge leaves do not mesh, loosen the screws slightly and tap the leaves into alignment.

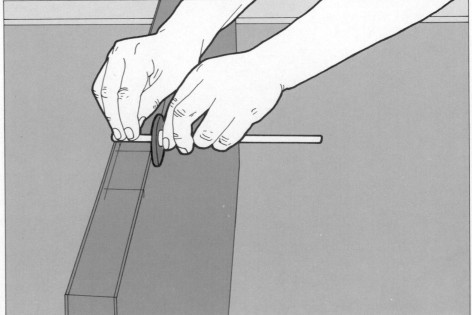

# Cutting Holes for a Lock

**1** **Aligning the holes.** Mark the lock-side edge of the door 36 inches above the floor and extend the mark across the edge and 3 inches across the side of the door that faces away from the stop. Fold the manufacturer's template supplied with your lock over the edge and face of the door, centered on the marked lines. With a pencil, mark the center of the doorknob hole on the face of the door and the center of the latch-bolt hole on the edge.

Shut the door and drill the knob hole with a hole saw; when the saw breaks through the door, stop drilling and complete the hole from the other side. Drive shims beneath the door to hold it open and drill the latch-bolt hole through the edge of the door and until it meets the knob hole.

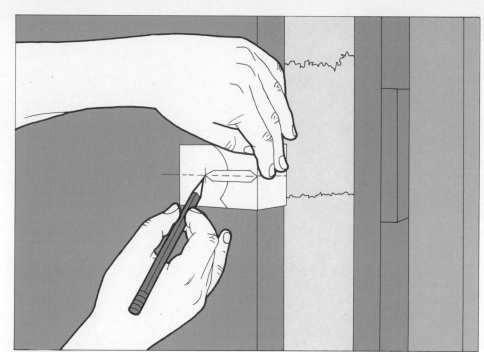

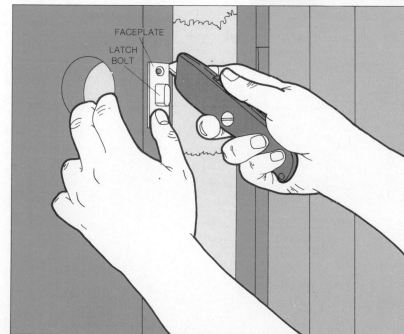

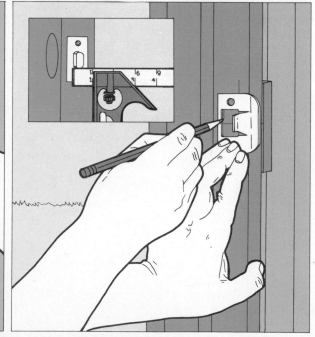

**2** **Mortising for the latch bolt.** Insert the barrel of the latch bolt in its hole, with the beveled edge of the bolt facing the doorstop, and outline the faceplate on the edge of the door with a utility knife. Chisel out a mortise as deep as the faceplate is thick (page 118, Step 6) and screw the latch-bolt plate to the door.

**3** **Locating the strike plate.** Measure from the face of the door nearest the stop to the flat side of the latch bolt (inset) with a combination square; measure the same distance on the jamb from the doorstop and mark a vertical line across the face of the jamb about 3 feet from the floor. Shut the door and transfer the 36-inch mark made in Step 1 to the jamb. Hold the strike plate against the jamb, centered on the 36-inch line, with the front edge of the plate's hole against the vertical line; mark the inside of the hole and the outside of the plate. Drill through the marked hole for the latch bolt, mortise for the strike plate and screw the plate to the jamb.

# Swinging Doors for Busy Passageways

The busy passageway between a kitchen and a dining room is best served by a door that can be pushed open from either direction and swings shut when released. Swinging doors come in full-sized or smaller café models, like those in Western-movie saloons. Both types can be hung in an existing finish frame with stops removed to permit the door to move in both directions.

Café doors are hung on pivot hinges, which allow the weight of the doors to swing them shut. A full-sized door, on the other hand, uses a spring-operated bottom hinge to close it. This is a bulky hinge, secured to both the floor and the bottom edge of the door, and requires modification of the door.

## A Full-sized Door

**1 Rounding the edges.** With the door secured in a door jack (page 121), scribe lines along each side of the door ¼ inch from its hinge-side edge, scribe a third line along the center of this edge and connect the three lines with arcs at the top and bottom edges. Then, using a jack plane, round off the edges to the arcs.

Repeat the procedure on the opposite edge of the door and sand both edges smooth.

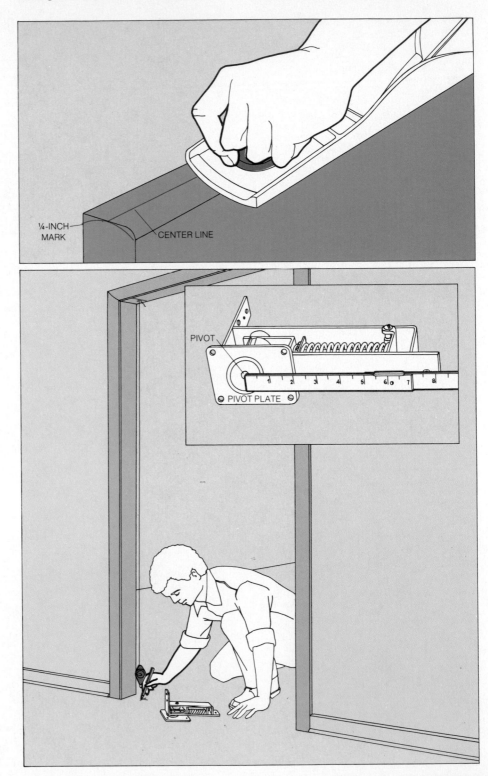

¼-INCH MARK

CENTER LINE

PIVOT

PIVOT PLATE

**2 Laying out the hinges.** On the head jamb, mark the top-pivot location at the distance from the hinge-side jamb specified by the hinge manufacturer and use a combination square to extend the mark across the width of the head jamb. Suspend a plumb line from the center of this line and measure the distance between the side jamb and the plumb line at the bottom and center of the side jamb; if the distance is less than that at the top, move the plumb line away from the side jamb until you obtain the required clearance. Mark the point where the plumb bob touches the floor.

Measure the distance from the center of the pivot to one end and one side of the pivot plate (inset). Mark the floor the same distances from the plumb-bob mark; align the pivot plate with these marks, centering it over the plumb-bob mark; and outline the plate on the floor.

**3 Installing the top pivots.** Drill a hole in the head jamb to fit the top-pivot cap at the location of the top pivot and insert the cap in the hole. Outline and mortise a recess for the wings of the cap as you would for the leaf of a standard hinge *(page 118)*, then turn the cap over and screw it to the jamb.

To locate the pivot socket in the top of the door, subtract the clearance between the door and the side jamb—specified by the pivot-hinge manufacturer—from the top-pivot measurement on the head jamb *(opposite, Step 2)*. Mark the location on a center line drawn along the top of the door, drill and mortise for the pivot socket and screw the socket to the door *(inset)*.

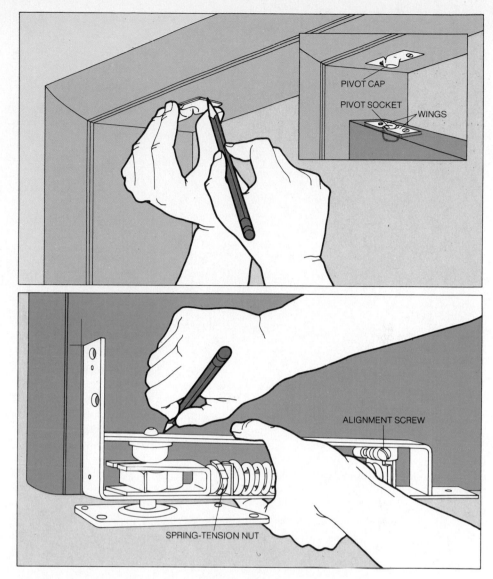

PIVOT CAP

PIVOT SOCKET — WINGS

**4 Mounting the floor hinge.** Starting at the bottom of the door, draw a line on the face of the door ½ inch from the hinge-side edge. Align the floor-hinge assembly with the line and the bottom of the door and outline the entire hinge with a pencil. At the top of the hinge, run a line across to the edge of the door. Use a handsaw and a chisel to cut out all the wood within the outline, set the hinge in the cutout and fasten it to the bottom of the door with wood screws.

With a helper, lift the door and fit the pivot socket over the pivot cap. At the bottom of the door, screw the pivot plate to the floor over the outline you made for it in Step 2. Center the door between the jambs by turning the alignment screw in the bottom hinge, and set the speed and force of the door's swing by adjusting the spring-tension nut. Finally, cover the hinge and the gap at the bottom corner of the door with the trim plates provided by the manufacturer.

ALIGNMENT SCREW

SPRING-TENSION NUT

## A Pair of Café Doors

**Installing gravity hinges.** Café doors are generally set about 12 inches above the floor, with gravity-pivot hinges at the top and bottom of each door. Each hinge consists of a jamb socket screwed to a side jamb and a pivot mounted on the top or bottom of the door; notches in the bottom hinge *(inset)* fit together to hold the door open. To install the doors, mount the bottom jamb socket, screw the pivots to the top and bottom of the door, slip the door into the bottom socket and then fit the top jamb socket over the top pivot and screw the socket to the jamb.

If the jambs are not plumb, plane the doors to fit—but only on the hinge sides. Otherwise, the doors will look lopsided because the center stiles will not be rectangular.

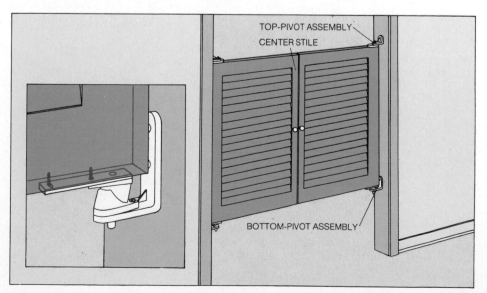

TOP-PIVOT ASSEMBLY

CENTER STILE

BOTTOM-PIVOT ASSEMBLY

## Picture Credits

The sources for the illustrations in this book are shown below. The drawings were created by Roger C. Essley, Fred Holz, Joan S. McGurren and Jeff Swarts. Credits for the pictures from left to right are separated by semicolons, from top to bottom by dashes.

Cover: Fred Maroon. 6: Fil Hunter. 8, 9: Whitman Studio, Inc. 10, 11: John Massey. 12 through 16: Peter McGinn. 17, 18: Whitman Studio, Inc. 21, 22: John Massey. 23 through 27: Peter McGinn. 28 through 39: Walter Hilmers Jr. 40 through 43: Peter McGinn. 44 through 49: John Massey. 50 through 55: Whitman Studio, Inc. 56: Fil Hunter. 58 through 65: Walter Hilmers Jr. 66 through 73: Frederic F. Bigio from B-C Graphics. 74: Fil Hunter. 76 through 87: Frederic F. Bigio from B-C Graphics. 88 through 95: Walter Hilmers Jr. 96: Fil Hunter. 98 through 106: Frederic F. Bigio from B-C Graphics. 107, 108, 109: Raymond Skibinski. 110 through 115: John Massey. 116 through 123: Gerry Gallagher. 124, 125: Eduino J. Pereira.

## Acknowledgments

The index/glossary for this book was prepared by Mel Ingber. The editors also wish to thank the following: Alexandria Glass Shop, Alexandria, Va.; Ron Alphin, Morgan Millwork Company, Alexandria, Va.; Kevin Arnold, James A. Hunter and Gary Swartz, Cub Run Builders, Alexandria, Va.; Jim Askins, Williamsport, Md.; Associated Building Components Company, Silver Spring, Md.; Richard Ayers, Overhead Door Company, Newington, Va.; Joseph Bagnulo, Arlington, Va.; Baldwin Hardware Manufacturing Company, Reading, Pa.; Ed Baughman, Huttig Sash and Door Company, Fredericksburg, Va.; Scott Bisch, Stanley Company, Door Systems Division, Birmingham, Mich.; Blaine Window Repair, Kensington, Md.; Estel Blankenship, Alexandria, Va.; William Borger, Washington, D.C.; French Bullington, Springfield, Va.; Dick Calamussi and Edward Reiss, Stanley Hardware, New Britain, Conn.; John and Gus Choporis, Silver Spring, Md.; Lawrence Claxton, Kern Distributors, Washington Grove, Md.; Robert Courtney, Arlington Woodworking and Lumber Company, Inc., McLean, Va.; J. Michael Cramer, Alexandria, Va.; Connie Curling, Door Systems, Inc., Lorton, Va.; Julian Curtis, Suitland, Md.; Discount Window Repair Service, Rockville, Md.; Dixie Sheet Metal Works, Falls Church, Va.; William Everard, Fire Prevention Bureau, City of Alexandria, Va.; Marvin Fedro, Ideal Manufacturing Co., Waco, Tex.; W. G. Foster, Charles Koncker and Jack Ullrich, Andersen Window Walls, Bayport, Minn.; Lawrence P. Galanter, PPG Industries, Inc., Pittsburgh, Pa.; James L. Guthrie, Sterling, Va.; Earl F. Harvey, Gaines Brothers, Inc., Alexandria, Va.; Harry P. Harwood, Alexandria, Va.; Don Hawkins, Washington, D.C.; Bill Heffner Jr. and Steve Schlegel, Pease Ever-Strait Door Systems, Fairfield, Ohio; Ralph Hendrickson, Heritage Home Improvement, Falls Church, Va.; Robert Hewett, National Forest Products Association, Washington, D.C.; Larry Hufty, Building Department, City of Alexandria, Va.; George Hunt, Hechinger Company, Washington, D.C.; William Jawish and Dick Lawall, John Ligon, Inc., Bethesda, Md.; Marilyn Jones, Consumer Affairs, U.S. Postal Service, Washington, D.C.; R. I. Kellogg and Daughters, Alexandria, Va.; Walter Kozlowski and Eugene Schweiss, W. T. Weaver & Sons, Inc., Washington, D.C.; James Lansburgh, Lansburgh Construction Corp., Arlington, Va.; C. R. McCalley, Alexandria, Va.; Michael Maffioli, Washington, D.C.; Chick Milam, Robert Montgomery, Ray Shortt and Evert West, Fairfax Lumber and Millwork Co., Inc., Alexandria, Va.; Frank Modica, Weyerhaeuser-Wood Products Division, Edison, N.J.; National Woodwork Manufacturer's Association, Chicago, Ill.; Nathaniel Neblett, National Trust for Historic Preservation, Washington, D.C.; R. Daniel Nicholson Jr., Rockville, Md.; Jim Papile, Woodworkers, Alexandria, Va.; James Pendleton, Good Earth Nursery, Falls Church, Va.; Buck Richardson, International Masonry Institute, Washington, D.C.; Myra Rodgers, Hires Turner Glass Co., Alexandria, Va.; Dale Schaefer, Del-Ray Rental, Alexandria, Va.; W. Flinn Settle, Bethesda, Md.; J. W. Sherin, Joanna Western Mills Co., Catonsville, Md.; Dave Slovick, Friday Associates, Philadelphia, Pa.; Jim Snodgrass, Wood Moulding and Millwork Producers, Portland, Ore.; Dennis Speisman, Mileham & King, Inc., Rockville, Md.; Bob Stoddard, New Home Custom Shades, Kensington, Md.; Tom Tucker, Pittsburgh Corning Corp., Radnor, Pa.; Charles Vernon, Del-Ray Glass and Mirror Company, Alexandria, Va.; Charlie Ward, Door Systems, Inc., Dunkirk, Md.; William F. Wiseman Jr., W. A. Smoot & Co., Inc., Alexandria, Va.

Sheila Galagan and Gretchen Wessels also provided assistance with the preparation of this book.

# Index/Glossary

*Included in this index are definitions of many of the technical terms used in this book. Page references in italics indicate an illustration of the subject mentioned.*

Apron: *interior trim below window sill.* Described, *8*, 19, *33*; replacing, *35-36*; shaping, *36*

Astragal: *strip used as stop between double doors.* Described, 19; use, 98

Brickmold: *exterior casing on door or window.* Described, *8*, 19, *33*; on prehung window, *76, 78*

Casing: *trim around inside and outside of door or window.* Described, *8*, 19, 28; installing, *29-31*; removing, *28*

Channels, window sash, *8*; cleaning, *10*; lubricating, *10*

Dado: *groove across width of board.* Described, 19, 88

Door, building and hanging, 97, 116; building finish frame, *116-119*; hanging, 116, *120-123*; hinges, 116, *117-118, 122*; installing finish frame, *119*; locks, 116, 123; prehung vs. custom-built, 97; styles of, 97

Door, double, 98; installing exterior, *101*

Door, exterior, 98; installing, *99-101*; installing double, *101*; preparing opening, 99

Door, garage, *111*; installing, *111-115*; preparing opening, *111*; springs, 111, *113-115*; structure, *110*

Door, interior hollow-core, 98; installing, *102*; patching, 20, 26; replacing, 116; split-jamb type, *98*

Door, interior solid-core, 98; installing, 98; replacing, *122-123*; uses, 98

Door, metal, repairing dents, 20

Door, prehung: *factory-preassembled door.* Described, 97, *98*; installing lock, *102*; installing new, *98-101*; types, 98

Door, repairing hinged: adjusting hinges, 20, *23*; latch alignment, 20, *23*; patching holes, *26*; planing, *24*; rattling, 20; removing, *24*; sagging, 20; sticking, 20; straightening jamb, 20, *24-26*; warped, 20

Door, sliding glass: adjusting, *106*; adjusting pocket-type, *109*; installing kit, *104-106*; installing pocket-type, *107-109*; pocket-type, 97, 104, 107; repairing, 27; types, 104

Door, swinging, 124; café, 124, *125*; hinges, *124-125*; installing full-sized, *124-125*

Door jack: *device that supports door for planing or repair.* Described, *121*

Door openings, framing: in balloon-type wall, 59, *63-65*; in brick veneer, *66-69*; in masonry, 66, *70-73*; in platform-type wall, 59, *60-62*. *See also* entries under Wall

Door and window trim, 28; casing, 28; installing casing, *29-31*; installing stops, *32*; removing casing, *28*; removing stops, *28*; stops, 28. *See also* Window trim

Drip cap: *protective flashing over door or window.* Installing on prehung window, *77, 78*

Frame, finish: *stationary frame around door or window.* Building for door, *116-119*; described, 19

Frame, rough: *framework around door or window opening.* Described, 19; in masonry walls, *73*

Glass: cutting curves, 6, 7, 50, *53*; cutting straight lines, 50, *51-52*; double-glazed panes, 50, 75, 88, 92; used in sliding doors, 104. *See also* Glazing

Glass block: installing, 49; replacing, 49

Glass cutter, 50; use, *51*

Glazing: *installation of glass panels.* Cutting glass, 50, *51-53*; double-glazed panes, 50, *55*; metal sash, *55*; preparing frame for, *50*; safe practice, 50; wooden sash, *54*

Glazing compound: *putty used to seal glass in frame.* Removing, *51*; types, 50

Glossary, 19

Header: *wood beam supporting load above door or window opening.* Described, 19, 56, *57*; dimensions, 59; sandwich, *59*; steel-reinforced, *59*

Hinges, door: for café doors, 124; installing, 116, *117-118, 122*; mortises, 20, 24; shimming, *23*; for swinging door, *124-125*; tightening, *23*

Jamb, door: *part of finish frame in which door swings or slides.* Building, *116-119*; lumber, 116

Jamb, window: *part of frame that holds window sash.* Described, *8-9*, 19; extension for prehung window, *77, 78, 79, 81*; straightening bowed, *10*

Kerf: *width of cut made by saw blade.* Described, 19

Light: *window or windowpane.* Described, 19

Lintel: *metal beam supporting load above opening in masonry wall.* Described, 19, 56, *57*; setting in brick-veneer wall, *66-68*; setting in solid-masonry wall, 66, 70; sizes, 66; types, 66, 70

Lock, door: fitting to door, *103*; installing in custom-built door, 116, *123*; structure, *103*; types, *103*

Lumber, shop: *kiln-dried pine.* Used for picture windows, 88

Miter: *angled edge cut for joining.* Described, 19

Mortise: *recess cut in one piece to hold another.* Described, 19, 97; making, for hinge, *117-118, 122*; making, for locks, 123

Mullion: *vertical trim between adjacent windows.* Described, 19

Muntin: *vertical or horizontal strip between windowpanes.* Described, *8*, 19, *37*; grille, 37

Muntin, repairing: horizontal, 37, *38*; vertical, 37, *39*

Needles: *temporary supports for openings in solid-masonry walls.* Described, 70, *71*; installing, *70-71, 72*

Operator: *crank assembly on casement and awning windows.* Cleaning and lubricating, 17; replacing, *17*

Parting strip: *strip separating sashes of double-hung window.* Described, *8*, 19

Plane: anatomy, *21*; block, 20, *21*; jack, 20, *21*; use, 20, 21, 22

Plate, sole: *bottom beam of wall frame.* Described, *58*

Plate, top: *top beam of wall frame.* Described, *58*

Pliers, glass: described, 50; use, *53*

Rabbet: *steplike notch cut in edge of piece.* Described, 19, 88

Rail: *horizontal member of doorframe or sash frame.* Described, *8*, 19, *37*

Roof for bay window, 83; installing, 83, *85-87*

Sash: *movable part of window.* Described, *8*, 19; dismantling and